FOR ORGANS, PIANOS & ELECTRONIC KEYBOARDS

E-Z PLAY TODAY

137

CHILDREN'S MOVIE HITS

CONTENTS

ISBN 978-0-634-02912-7

HAL•LEONARD®
CORPORATION

7777 W. BLUEMOUND RD. P.O. BOX 13819 MILWAUKEE, WI 53213

Visit Hal Leonard Online at
www.halleonard.com

T0045013

The Bare Necessities

from Walt Disney's THE JUNGLE BOOK

Registration 4
Rhythm: Fox Trot or Swing

Words and Music by
Terry Gilkyson

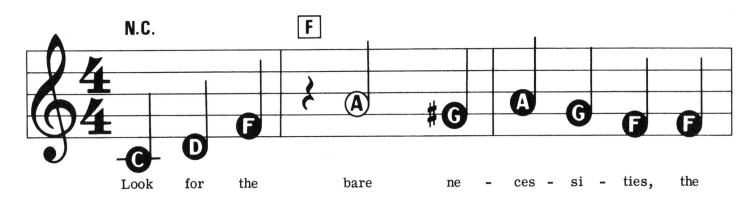

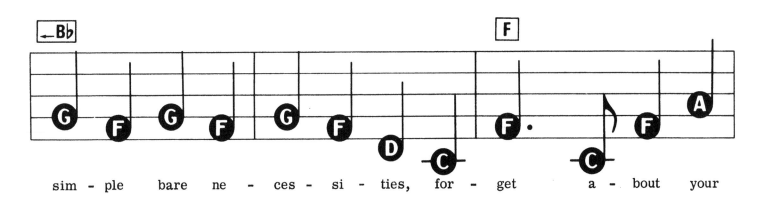

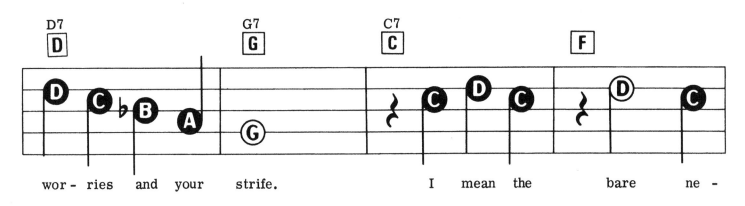

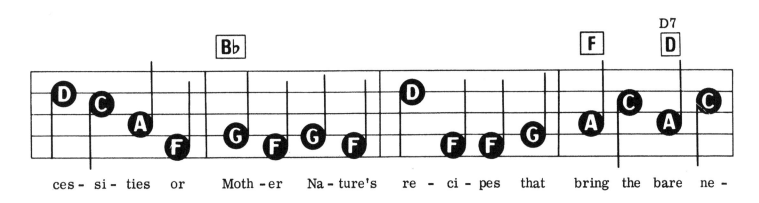

3

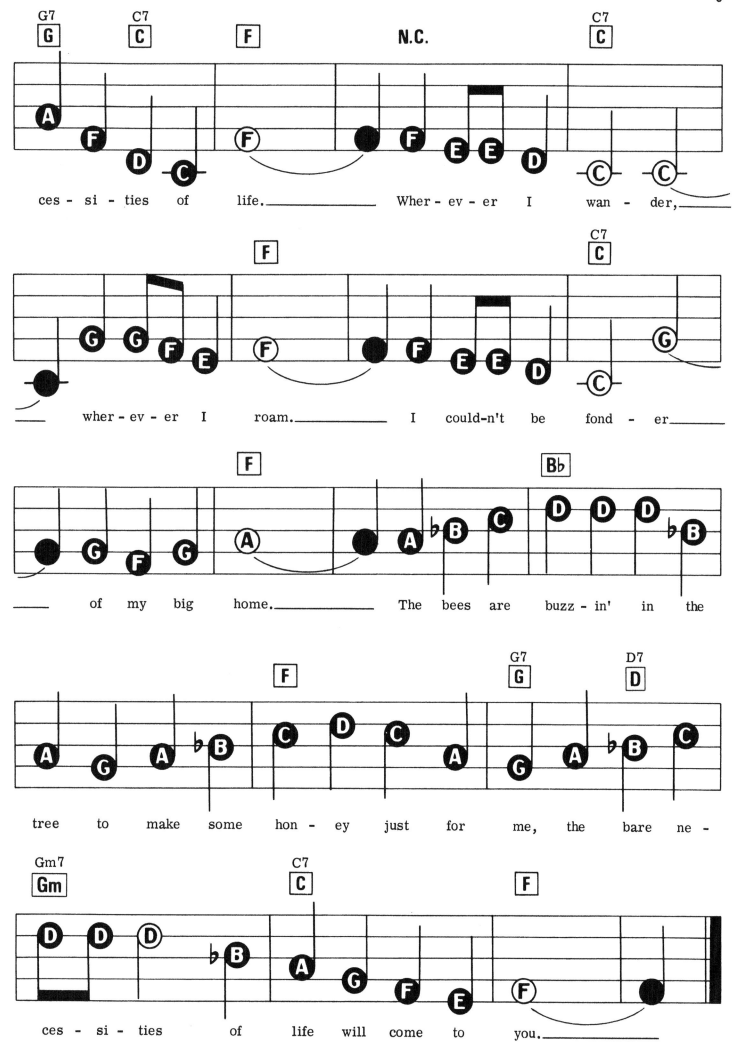

Beauty and the Beast

from Walt Disney's BEAUTY AND THE BEAST

Registration 1
Rhythm: Pops or 8 Beat

Lyrics by Howard Ashman
Music by Alan Menken

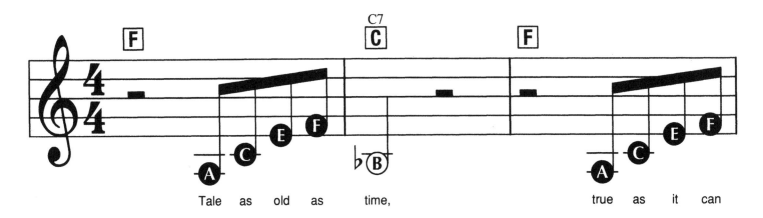

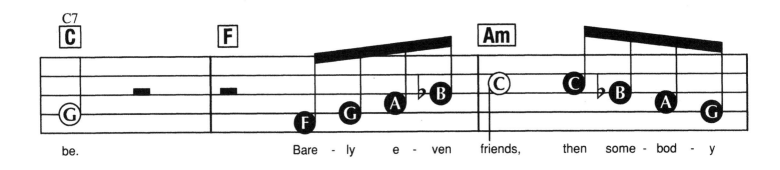

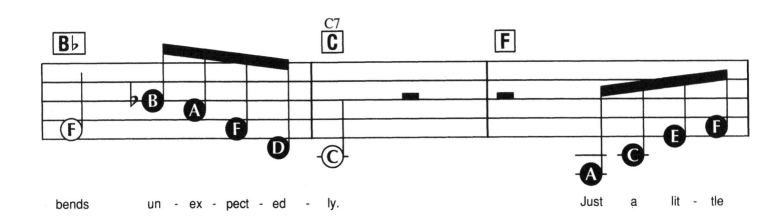

5

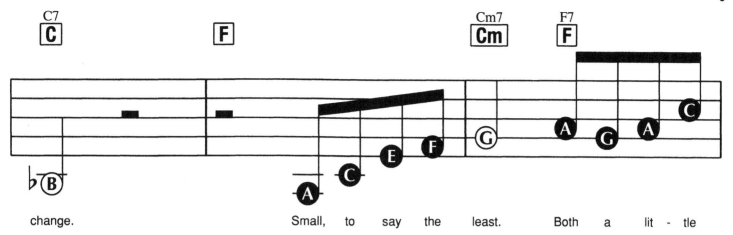

change.   Small, to say the least. Both a lit - tle

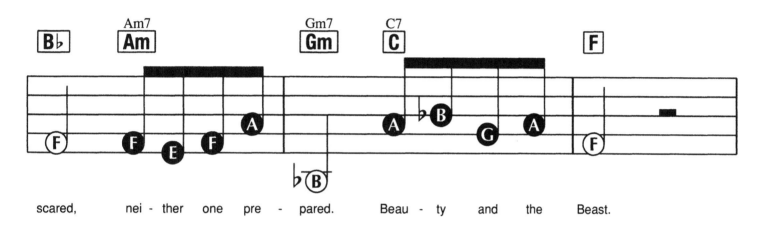

scared, nei - ther one pre - pared. Beau - ty and the Beast.

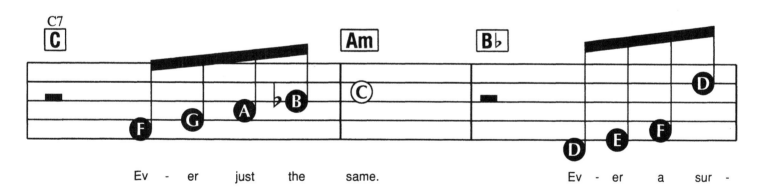

Ev - er just the same.   Ev - er a sur -

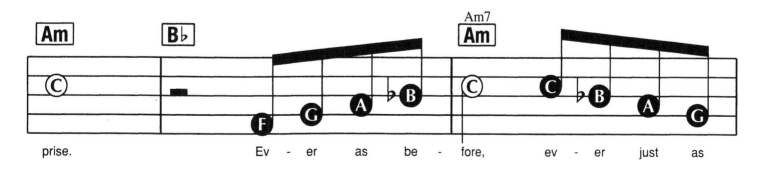

prise.   Ev - er as be - fore, ev - er just as

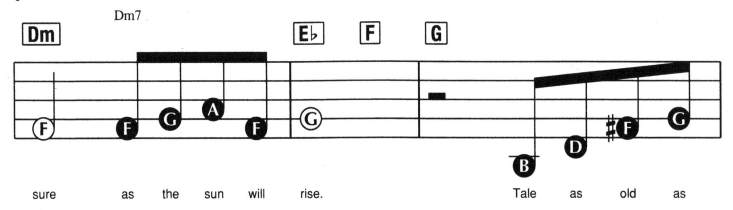

sure   as   the   sun   will   rise.   Tale   as   old   as

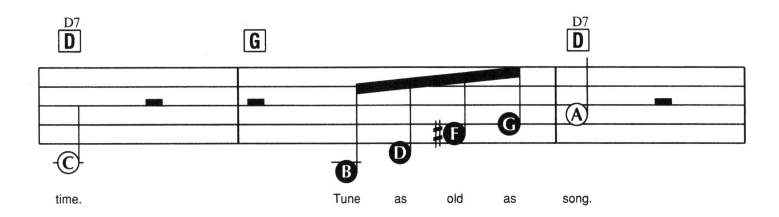

time.   Tune   as   old   as   song.

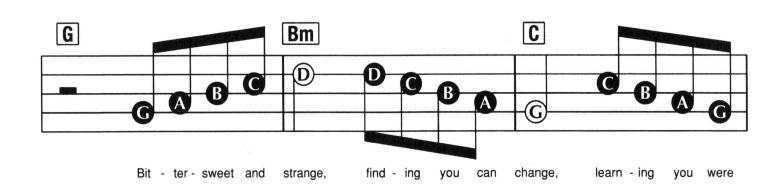

Bit - ter - sweet   and   strange,   find - ing   you   can   change,   learn - ing   you   were

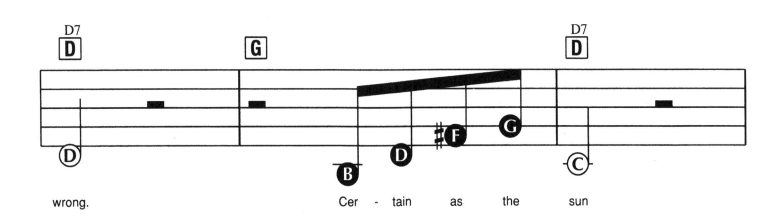

wrong.   Cer - tain   as   the   sun

7

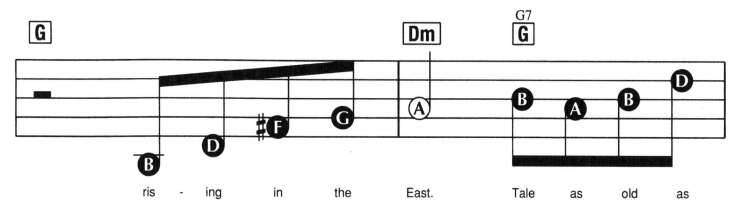

ris - ing in the East. Tale as old as

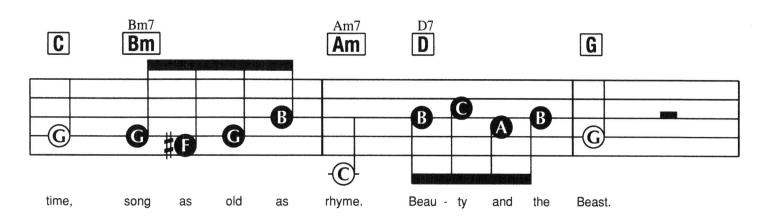

time, song as old as rhyme. Beau - ty and the Beast.

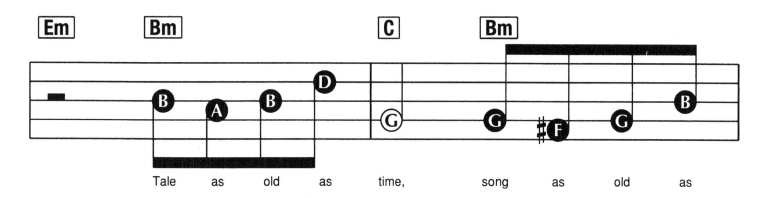

Tale as old as time, song as old as

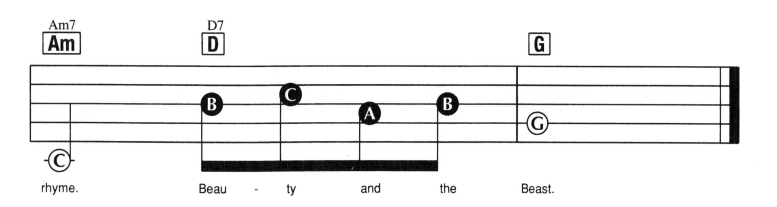

rhyme. Beau - ty and the Beast.

Bibbidi-Bobbidi-Boo
(The Magic Song)
from Walt Disney's CINDERELLA

Registration 8
Rhythm: Swing

Words by Jerry Livingston
Music by Mack David and Al Hoffman

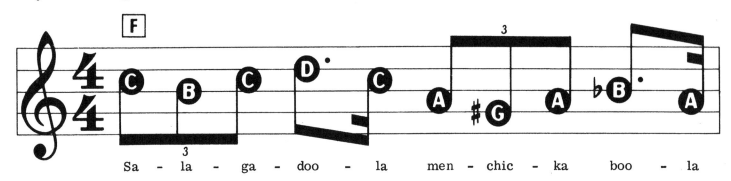

Sa - la - ga - doo - la men - chic - ka boo - la

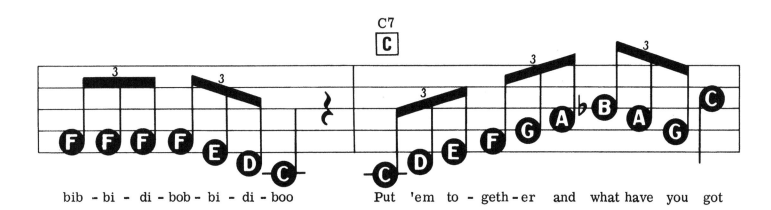

bib - bi - di - bob - bi - di - boo   Put 'em to - geth - er and what have you got

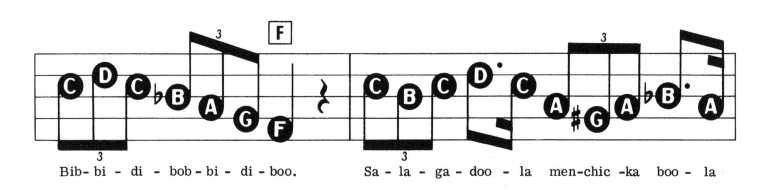

Bib - bi - di - bob - bi - di - boo.   Sa - la - ga - doo - la men - chic - ka boo - la

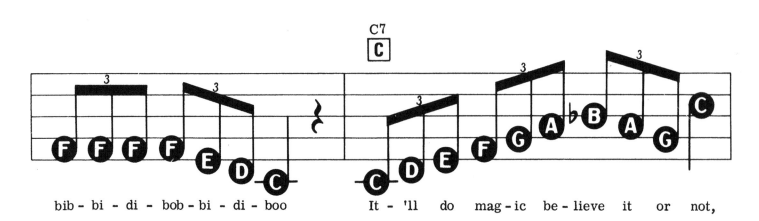

bib - bi - di - bob - bi - di - boo   It - 'll do mag - ic be - lieve it or not,

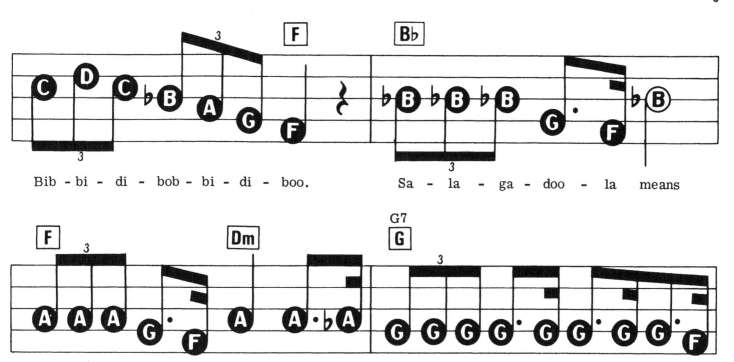

Bib - bi - di - bob - bi - di - boo.   Sa - la - ga - doo - la means

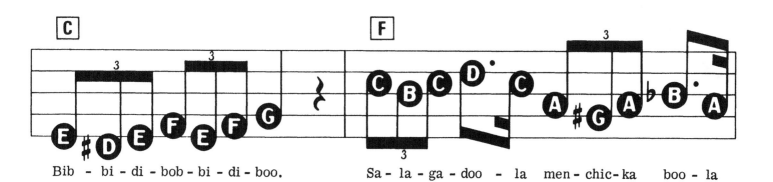

men-chic- ka boo - le - roo,   But   the   thing - a - ma-bob   that does   the   job   is

Bib - bi - di - bob - bi - di - boo.   Sa - la - ga - doo - la men - chic-ka   boo - la

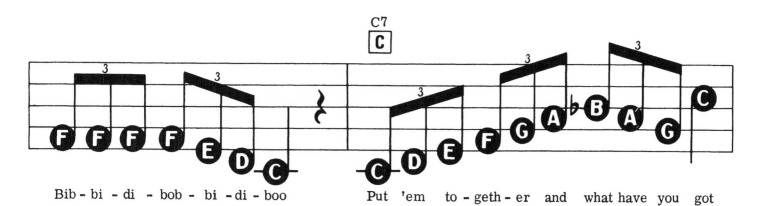

Bib - bi - di - bob - bi - di - boo   Put 'em to-geth - er   and   what have you   got

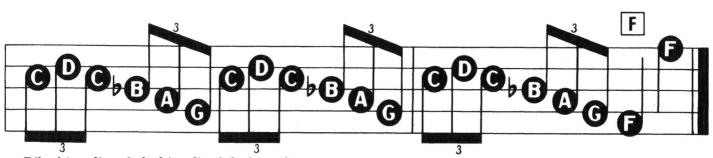

Bib- bi - di - bob-bi - di - bib-bi - di - bob-bi - di   Bib-bi - di - bob-bi - di - boo.

Candle on the Water
from Walt Disney's PETE'S DRAGON

Registration 1
Rhythm: Fox Trot or Ballad

Words and Music by Al Kasha
and Joel Hirschhorn

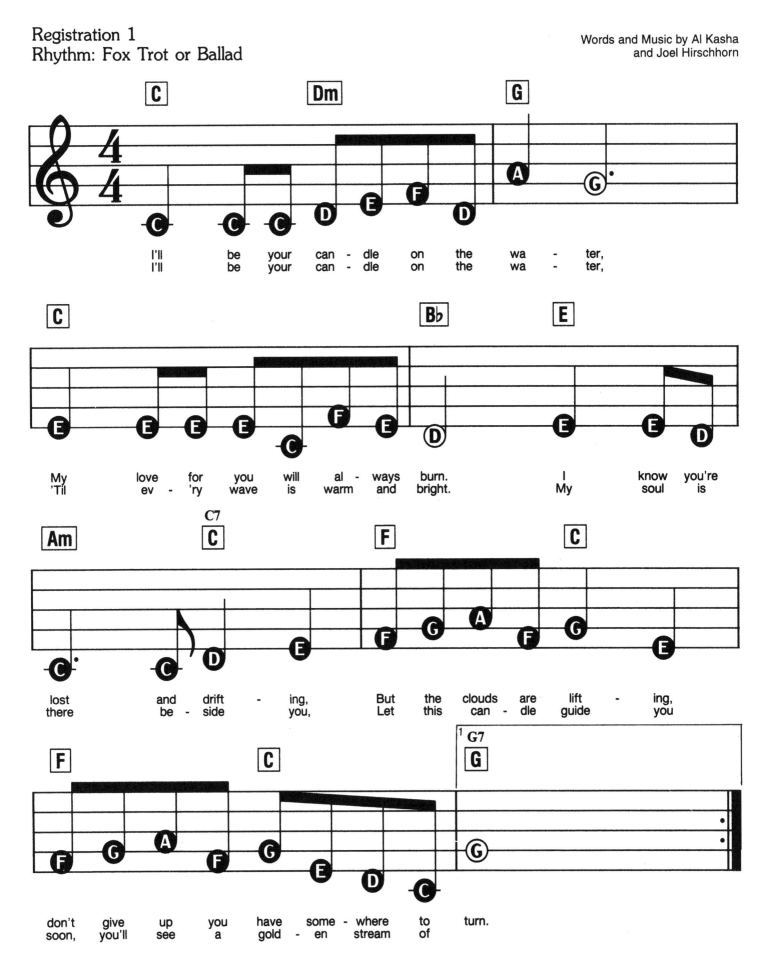

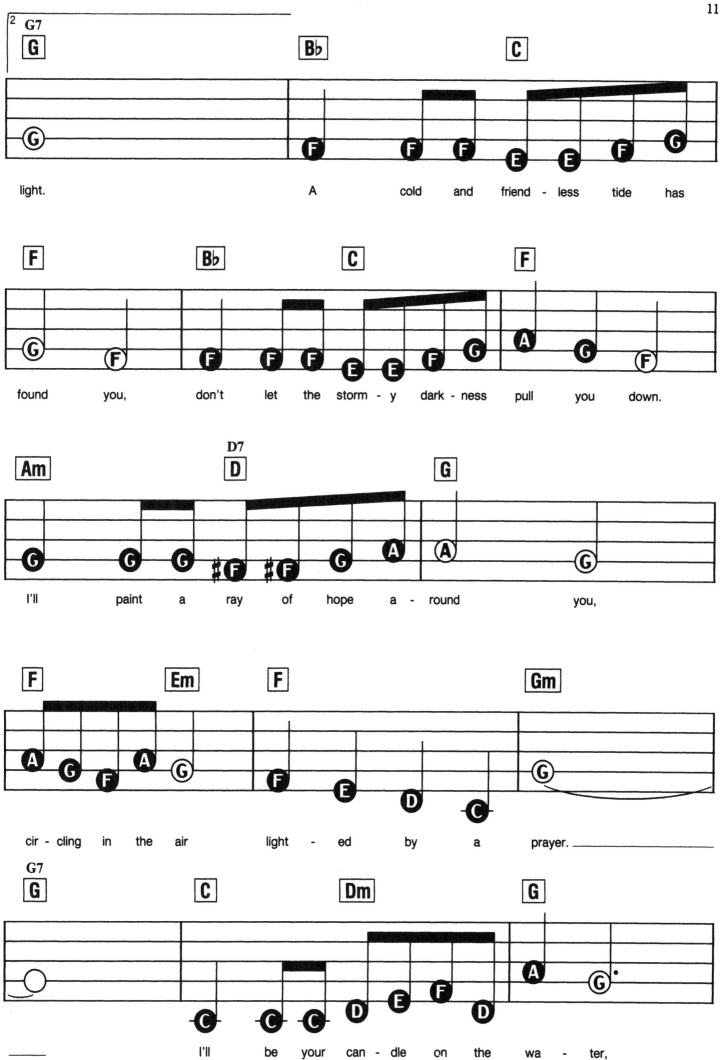

Hakuna Matata
from Walt Disney Pictures' THE LION KING

Registration 5
Rhythm: Swing

Music by Elton John
Lyrics by Tim Rice

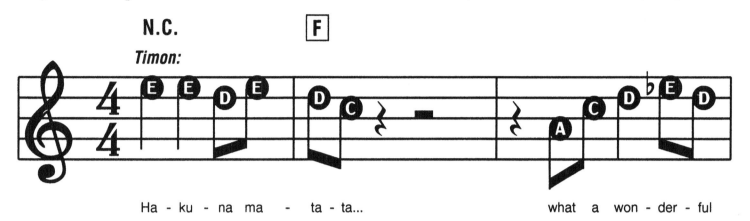

Ha - ku - na ma - ta - ta... what a won - der - ful

phrase! Ha - ku - na ma - ta - ta...

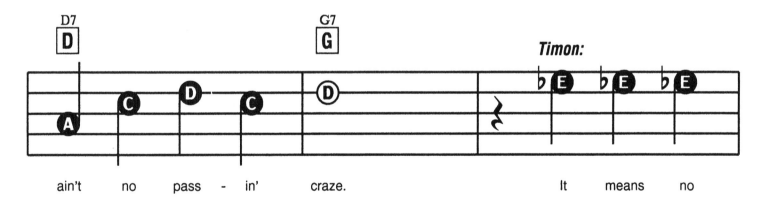

ain't no pass - in' craze. It means no

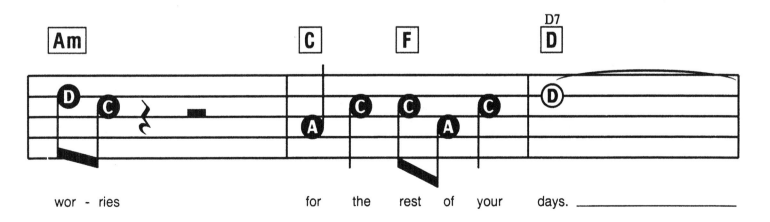

wor - ries for the rest of your days. _____

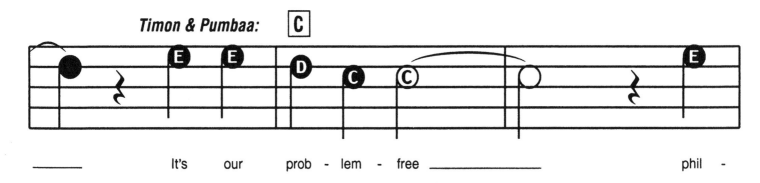

It's our prob - lem - free _____ phil -

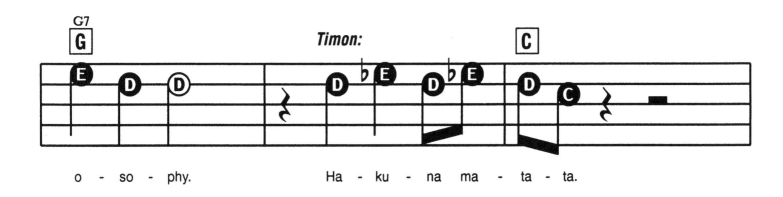

o - so - phy.   Ha - ku - na ma - ta - ta.

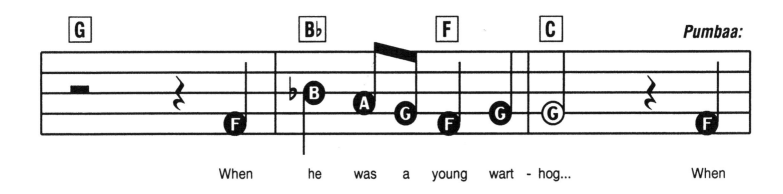

When   he   was   a   young   wart - hog...   When

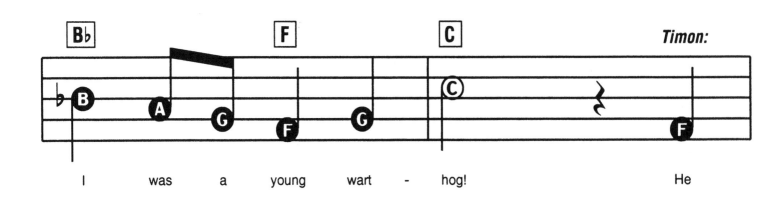

I   was   a   young   wart - hog!   He

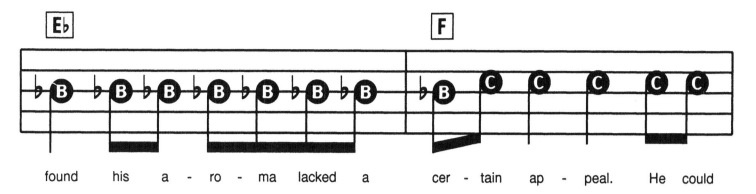

found his a - ro - ma lacked a cer - tain ap - peal. He could

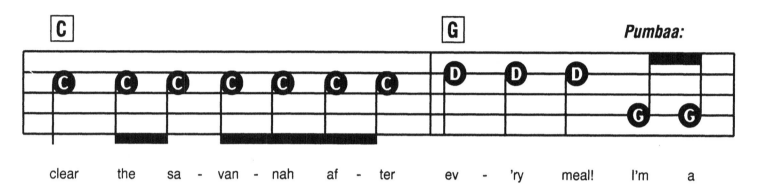

clear the sa - van - nah af - ter ev - 'ry meal! I'm a

Pumbaa:

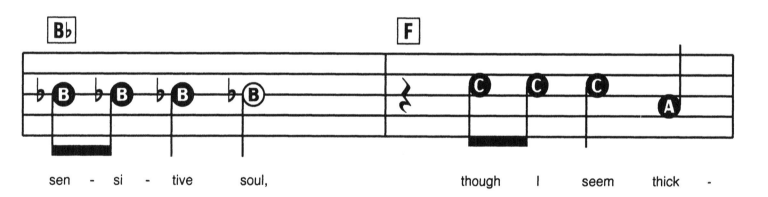

sen - si - tive soul, though I seem thick -

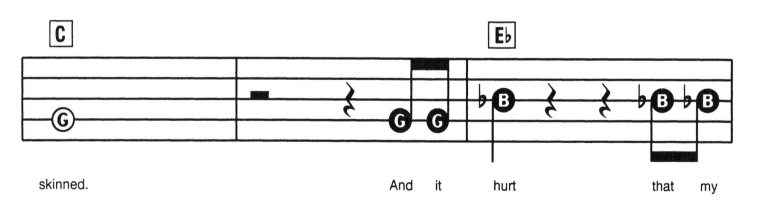

skinned. And it hurt that my

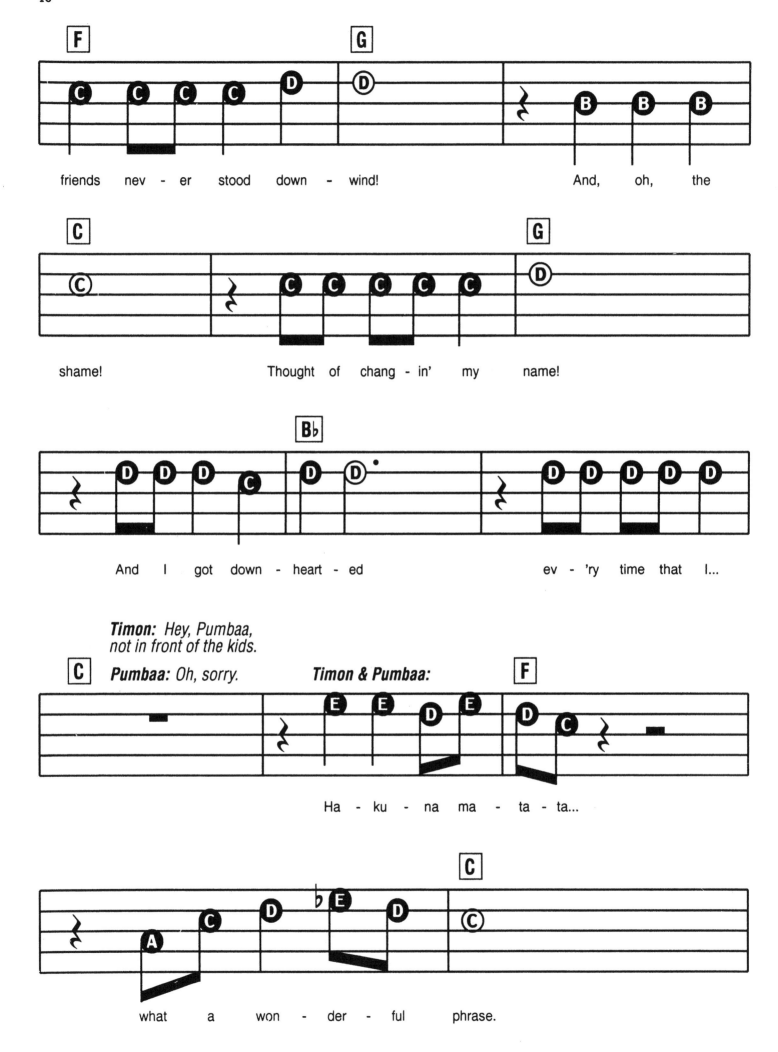

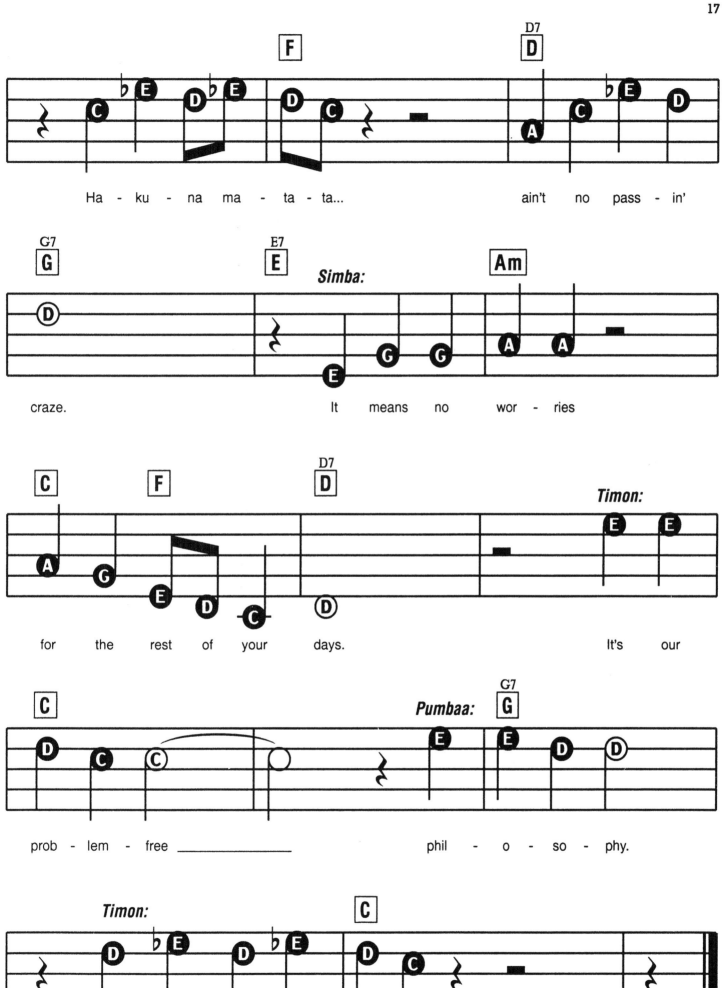

Chim Chim Cher-ee

from Walt Disney's MARY POPPINS

Registration 3
Rhythm: Waltz

Words and Music by Richard M. Sherman
and Robert B. Sherman

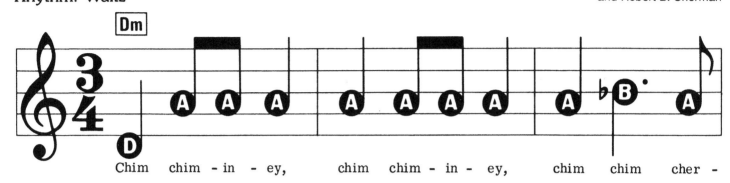

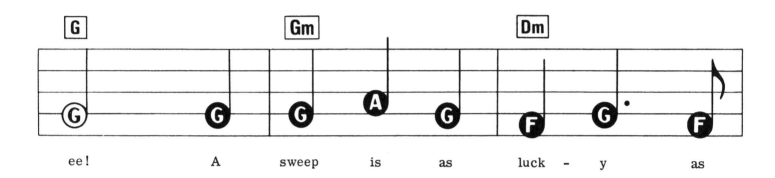

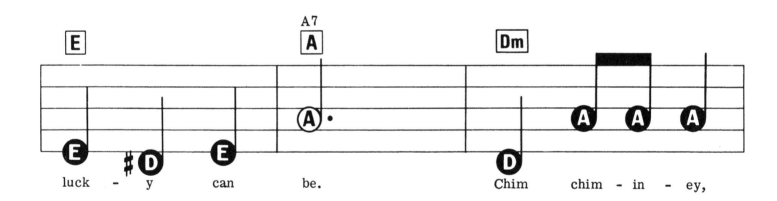

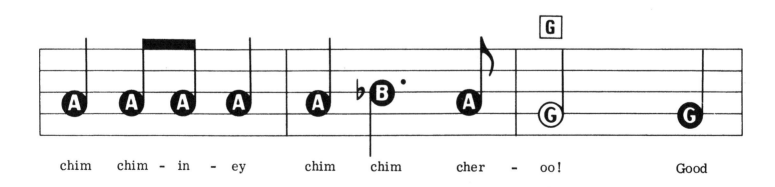

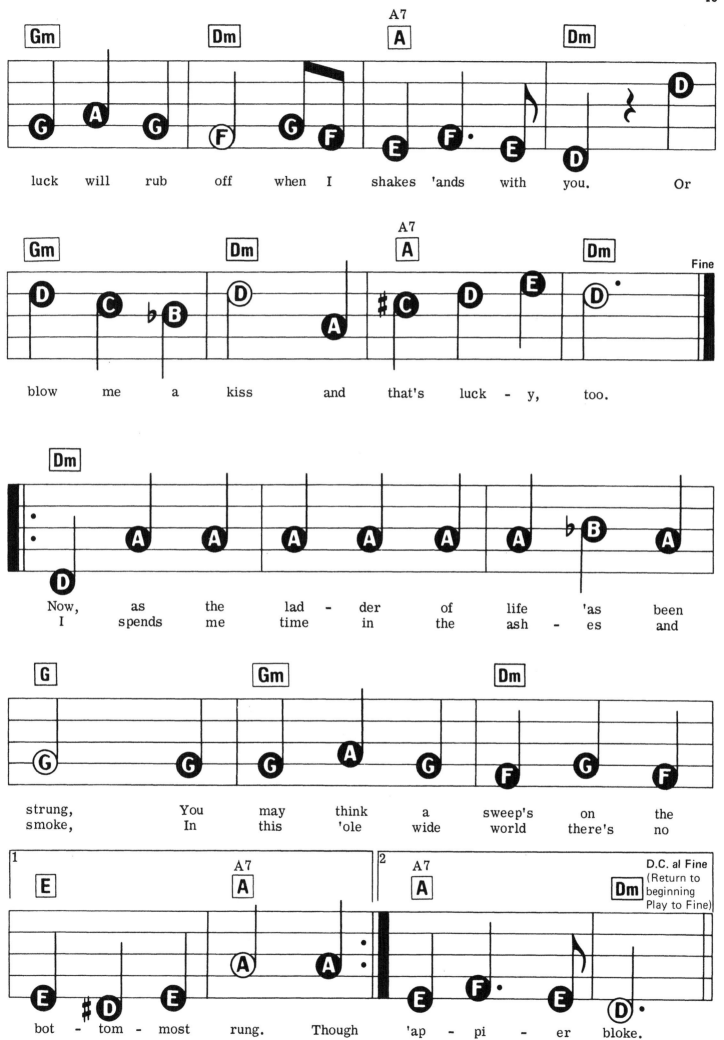

Do-Re-Mi
from THE SOUND OF MUSIC

Registration 4
Rhythm: March

Lyrics by Oscar Hammerstein II
Music by Richard Rodgers

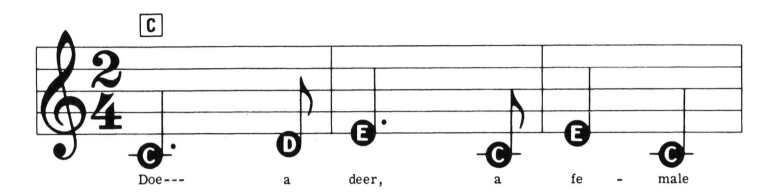

Doe--- a deer, a fe - male

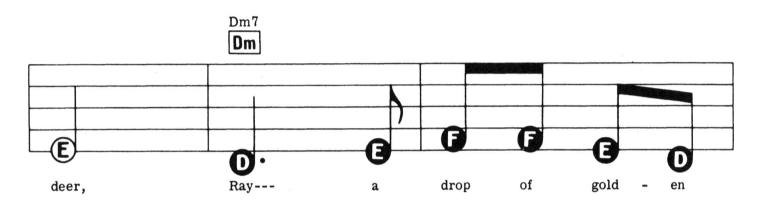

deer, Ray--- a drop of gold - en

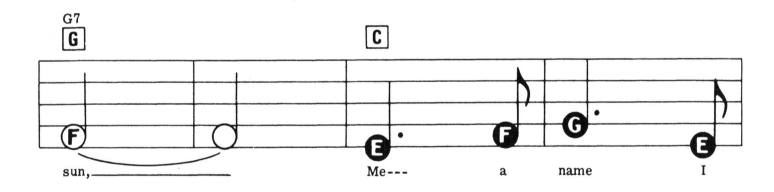

sun,_____ Me--- a name I

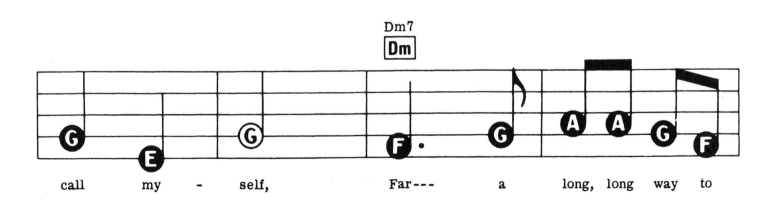

call my - self, Far--- a long, long way to

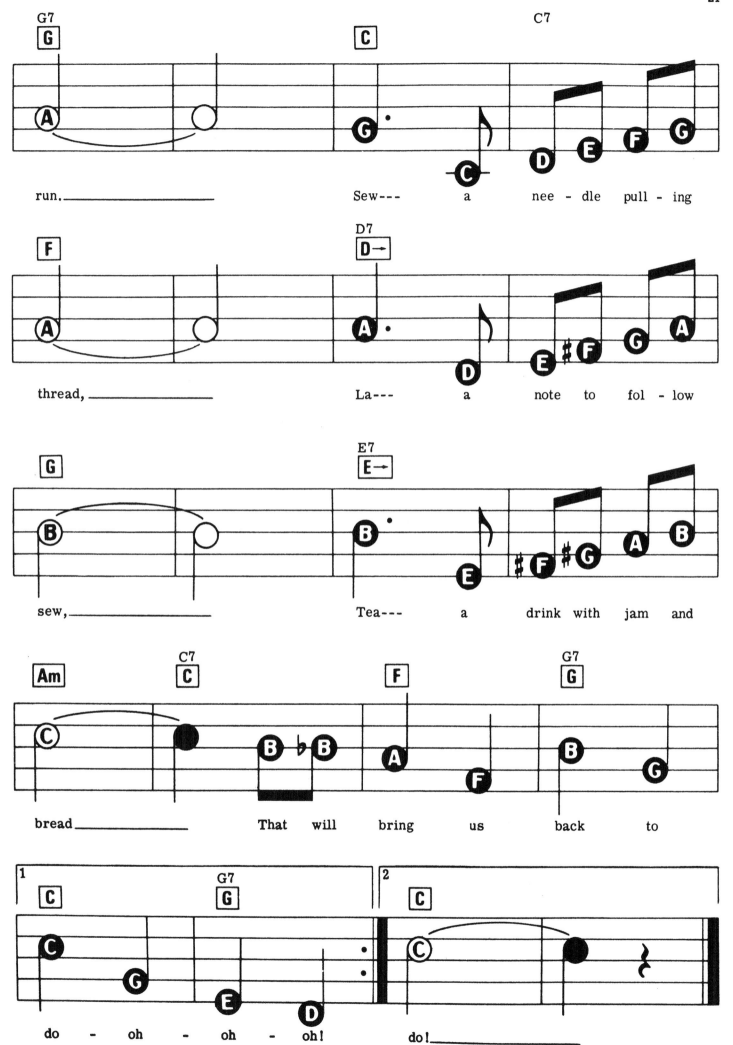

A Dream Is a Wish
Your Heart Makes
from Walt Disney's CINDERELLA

Registration 1
Rhythm: Ballad or Fox Trot

Words and Music by Mack David,
Al Hoffman and Jerry Livingston

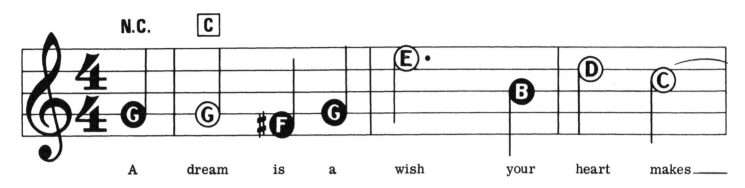

A dream is a wish your heart makes____

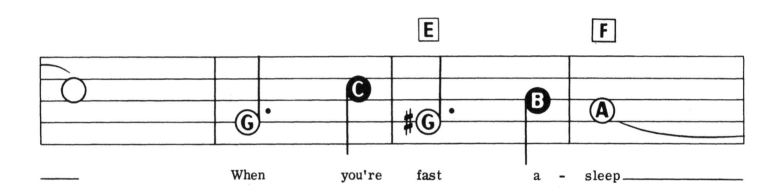

____ When you're fast a - sleep____

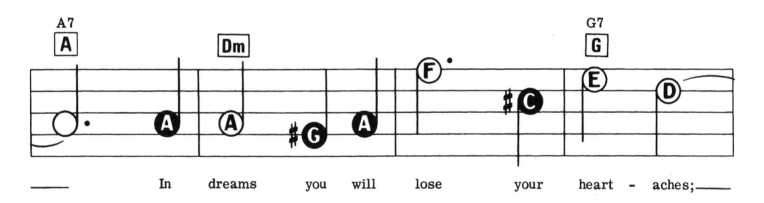

____ In dreams you will lose your heart - aches;

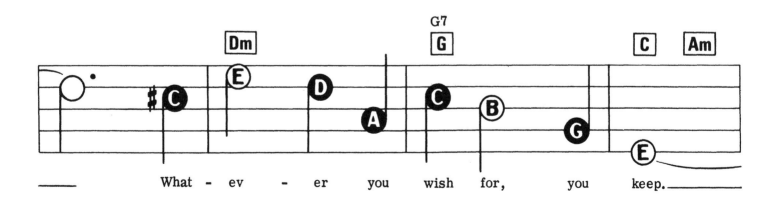

____ What - ev - er you wish for, you keep.____

23

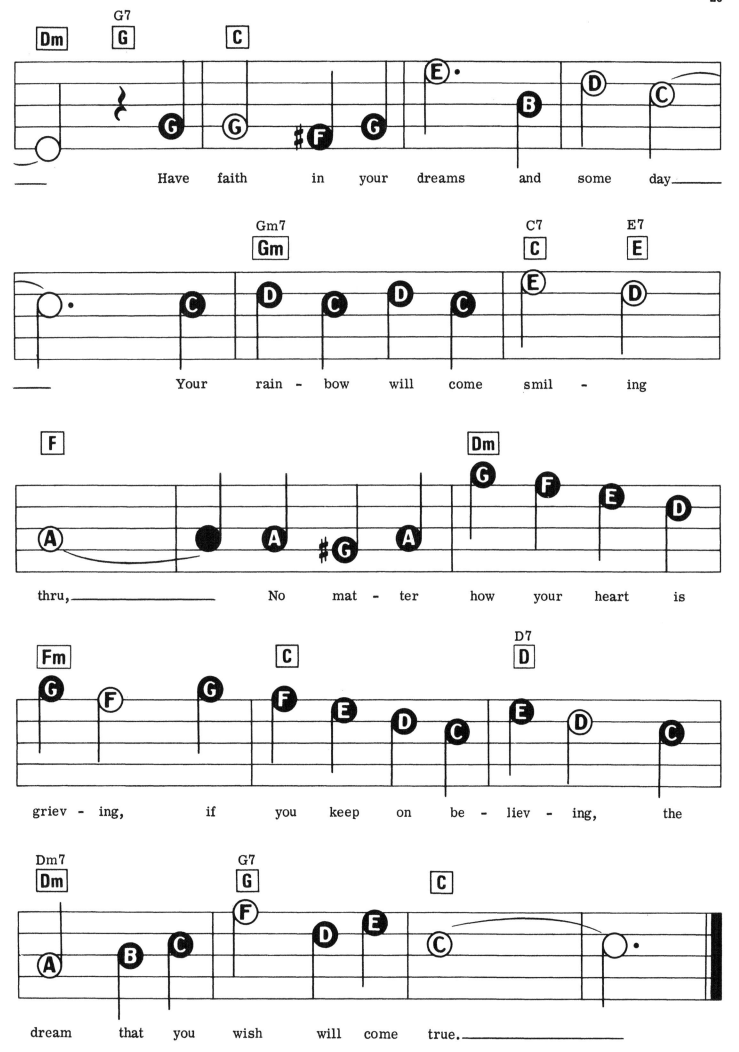

My Favorite Things
from THE SOUND OF MUSIC

Registration 9
Rhythm: Waltz

Lyrics by Oscar Hammerstein II
Music by Richard Rodgers

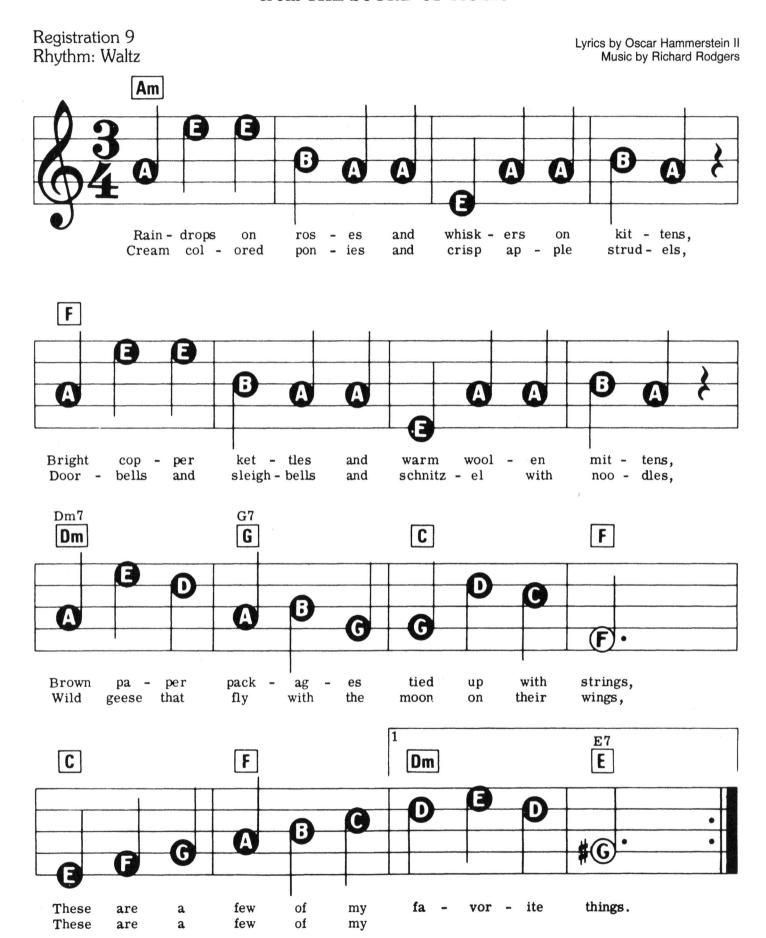

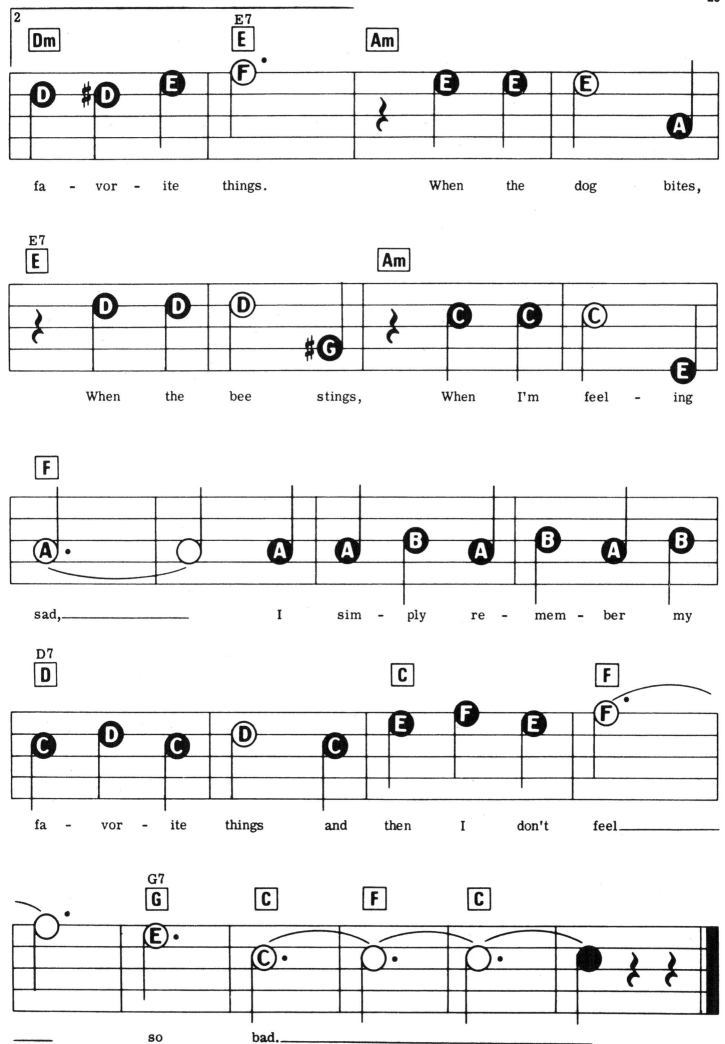

Raiders March
from the Paramount Motion Picture
RAIDERS OF THE LOST ARK

Music by John Williams

Registration 4
Rhythm: March

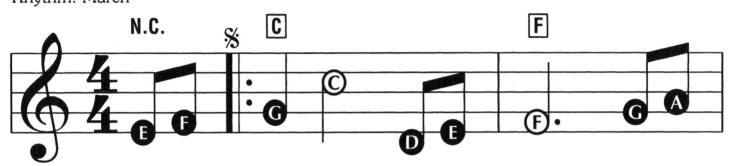

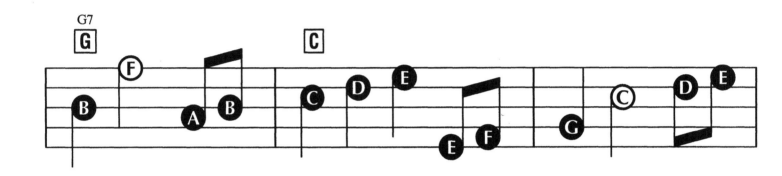

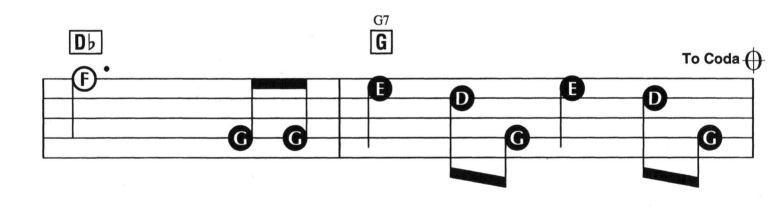

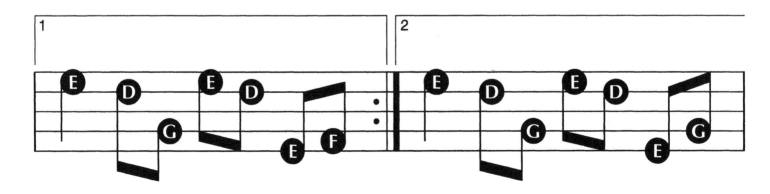

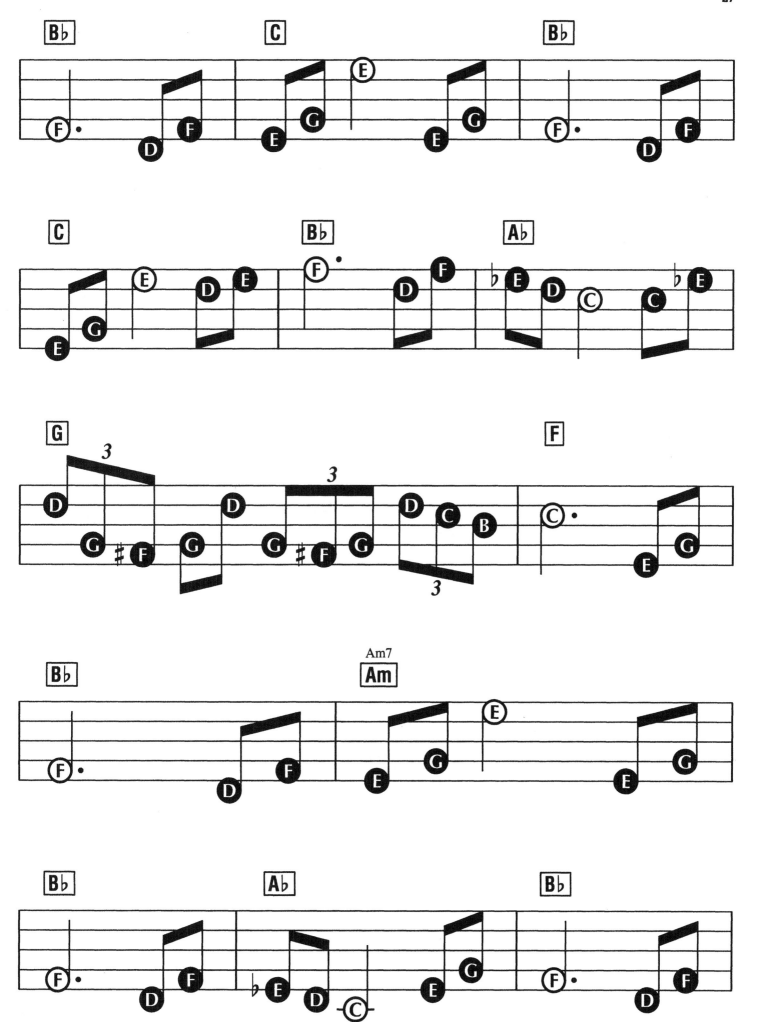

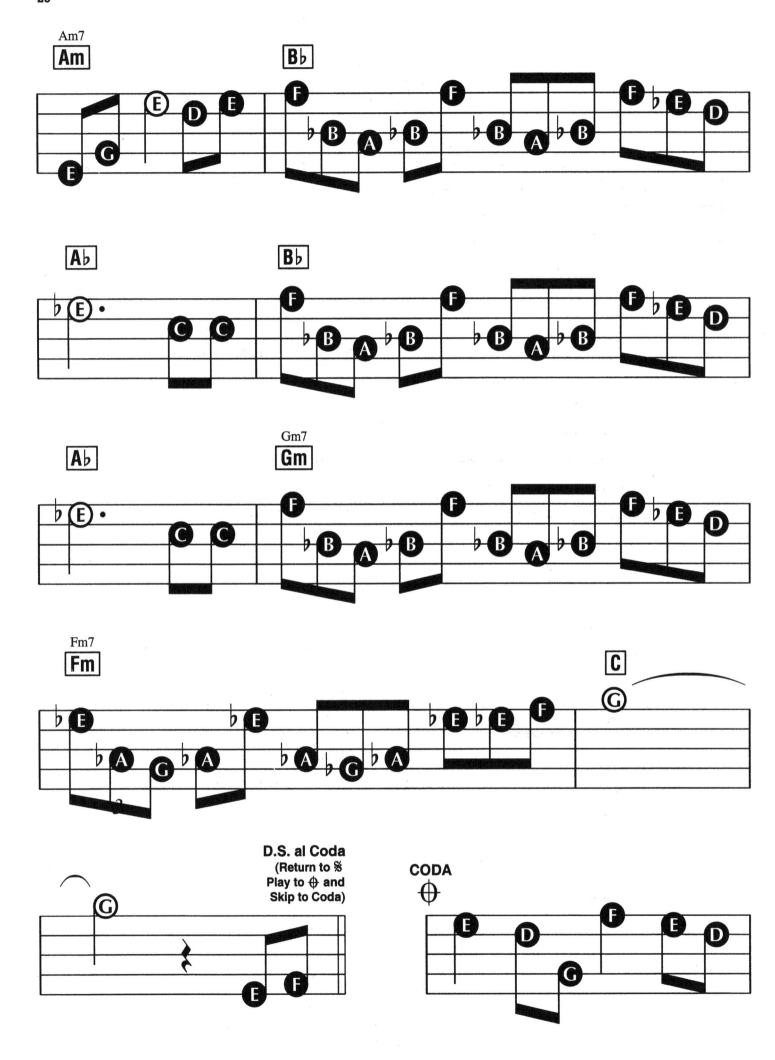

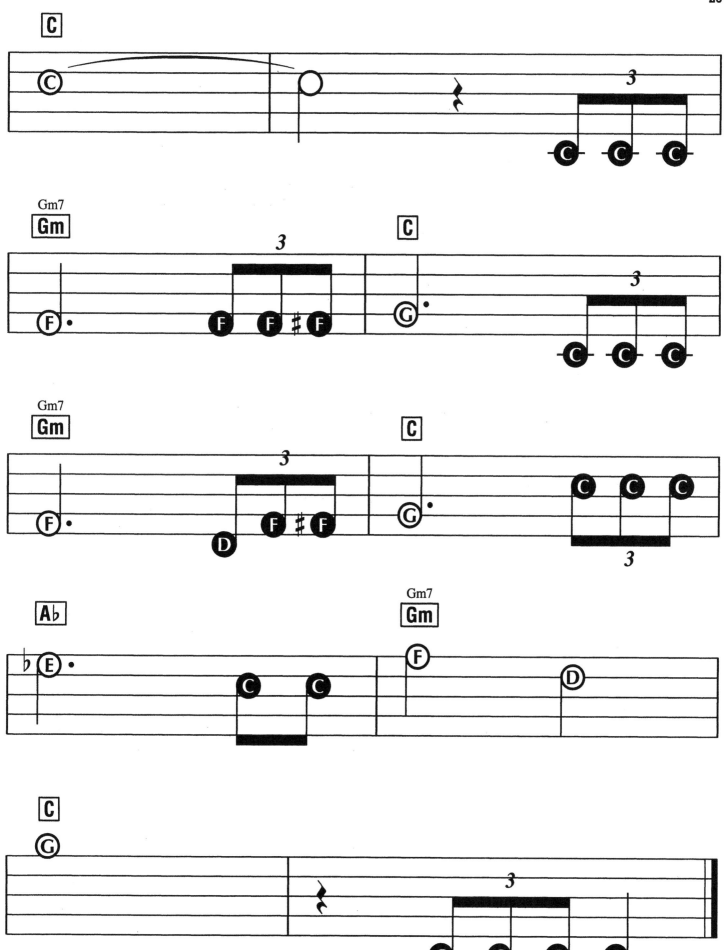

The Rainbow Connection
from THE MUPPET MOVIE

Registration 4
Rhythm: Waltz

Words and Music by Paul Williams
and Kenneth L. Ascher

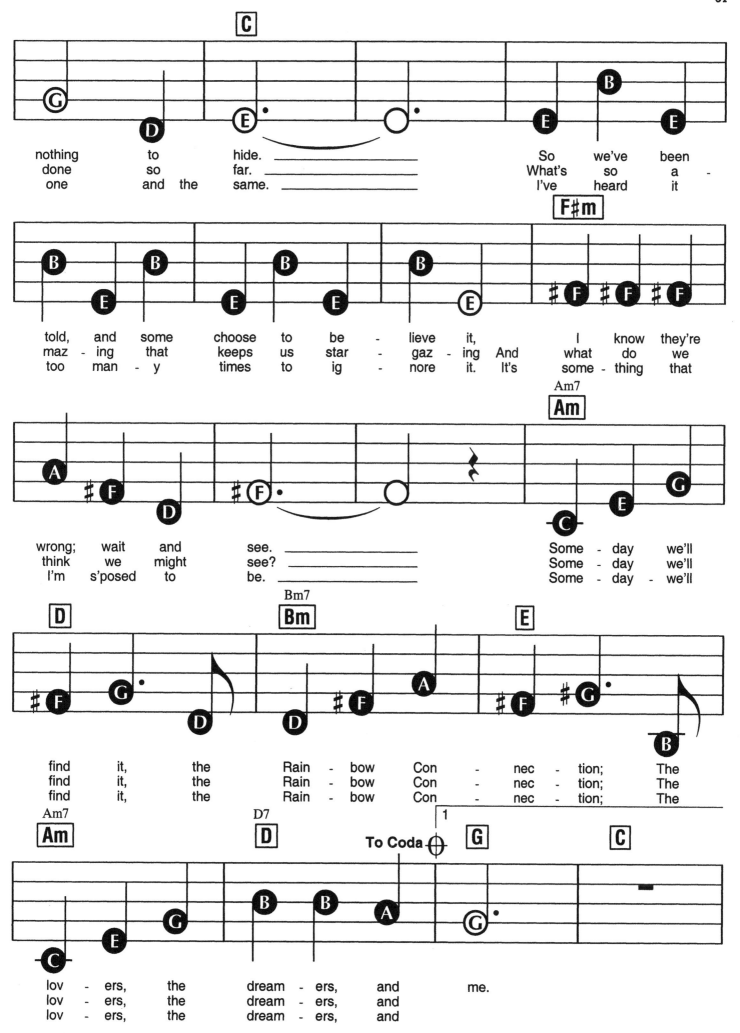

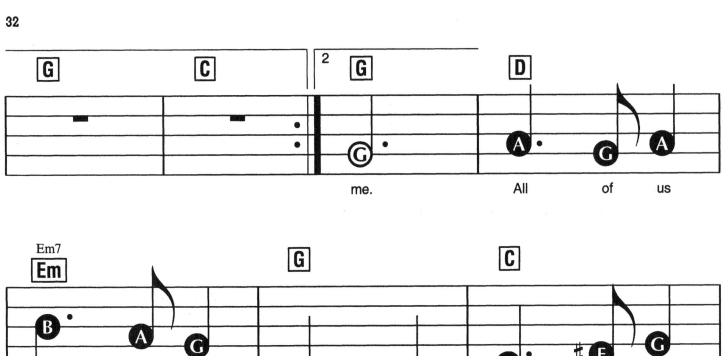

me.

All of us

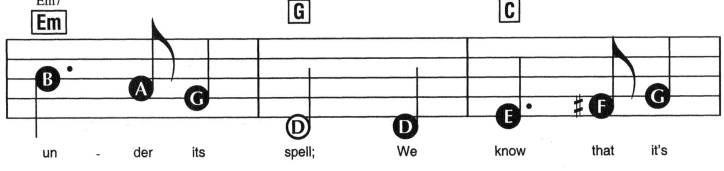

un - der its spell; We know that it's

D.C. al Coda
(Return to beginning
Play to ⊕ and
Skip to Coda)

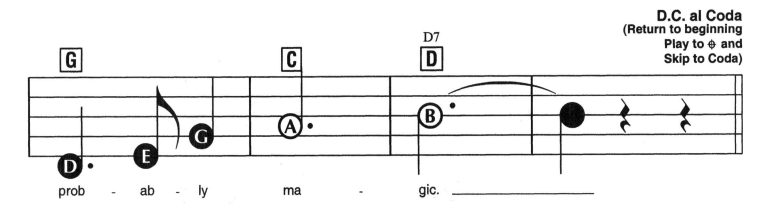

prob - ab - ly ma - gic. _____

CODA

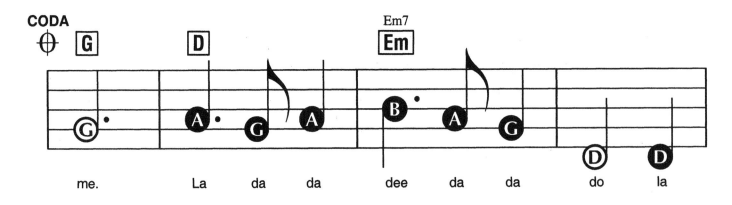

me. La da da dee da da do la

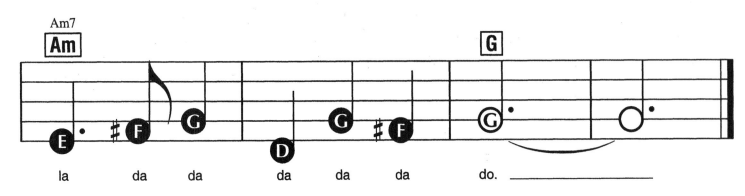

la da da da da da do. _____

Star Trek® the Motion Picture
Theme from the Paramount Picture STAR TREK: THE MOTION PICTURE

Registration 4
Rhythm: Shuffle

Music by Jerry Goldsmith

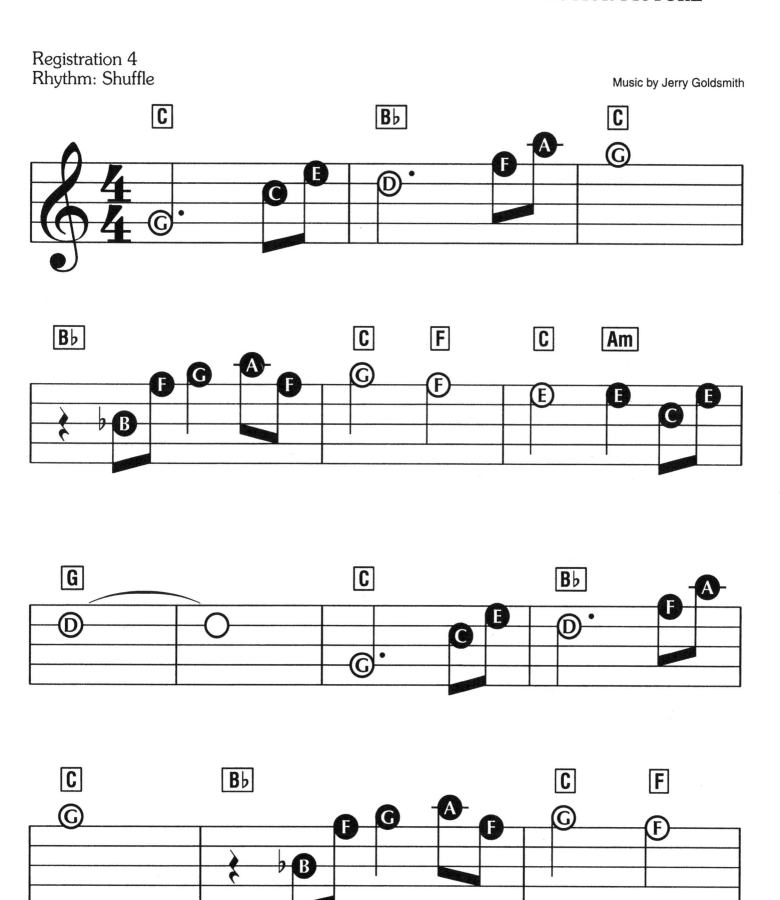

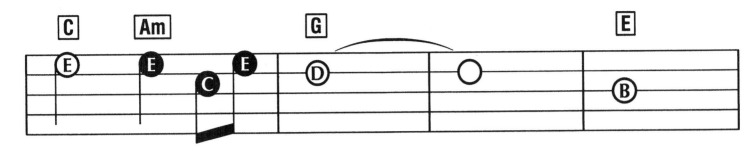

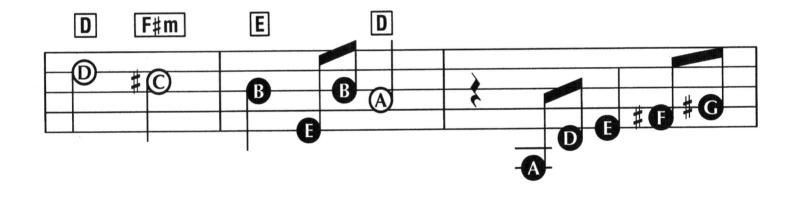

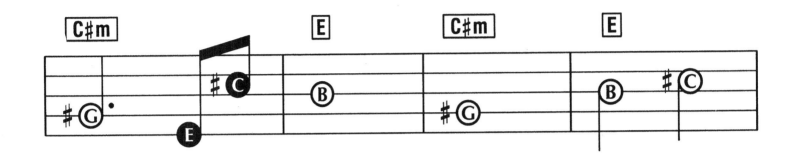

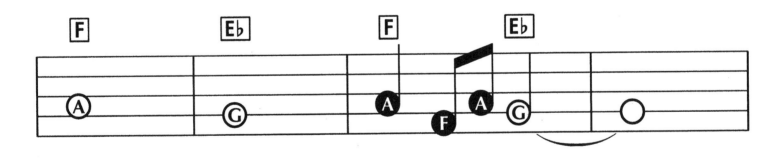

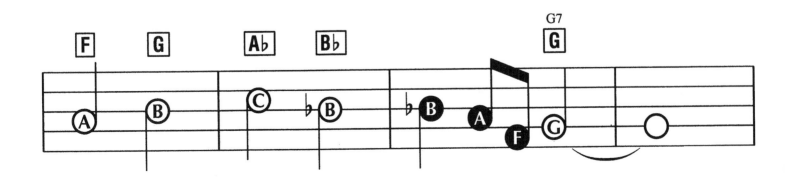

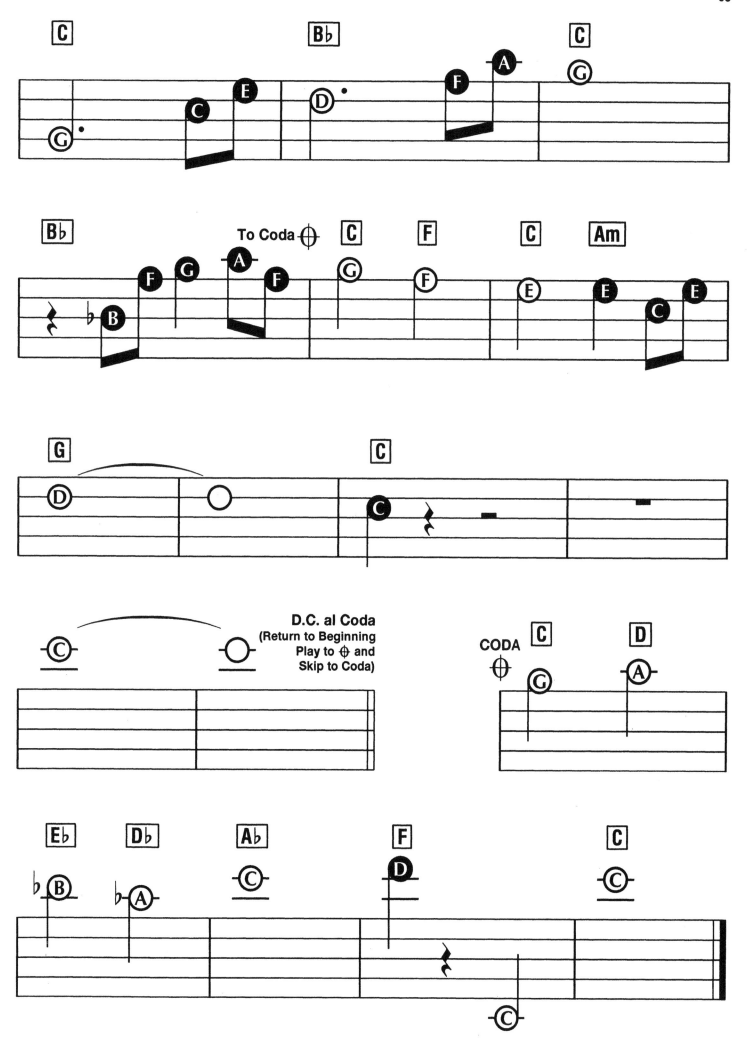

Someday
from Walt Disney's THE HUNCHBACK OF NOTRE DAME

Registration 1
Rhythm: Waltz

Music by Alan Menken
Lyrics by Stephen Schwartz

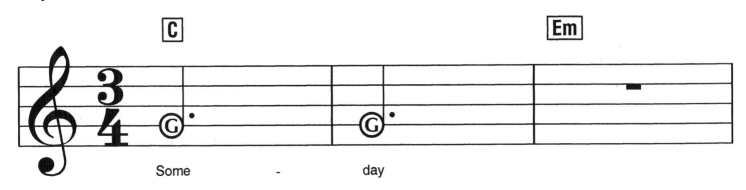

Some - day

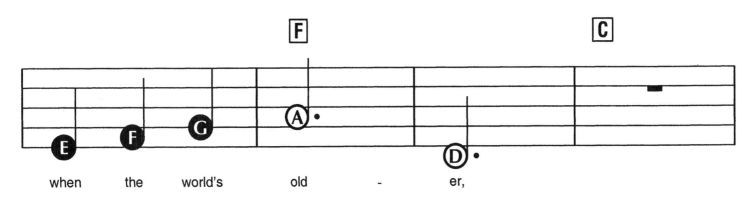

when we are wis - er,

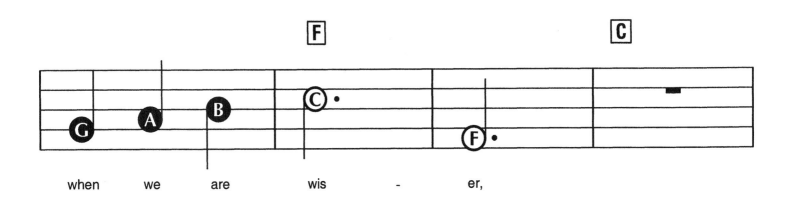

when the world's old - er,

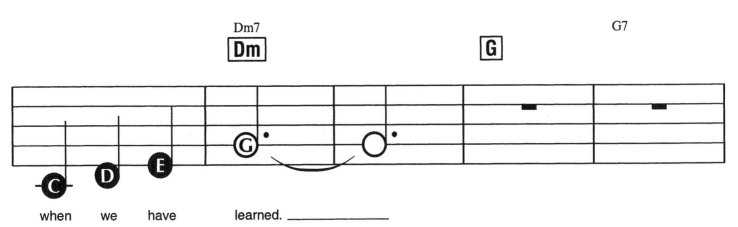

when we have learned. _____

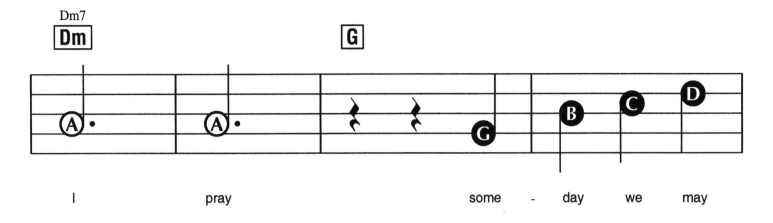

I   pray   some - day we may

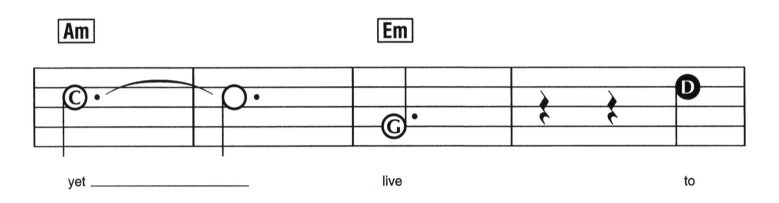

yet _____   live   to

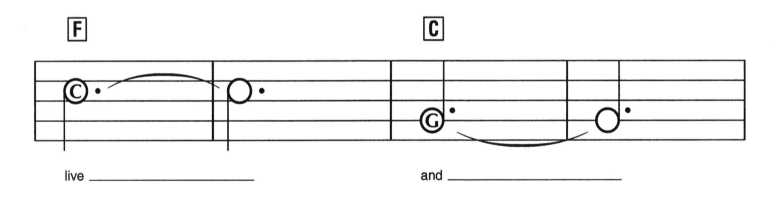

live _____   and _____

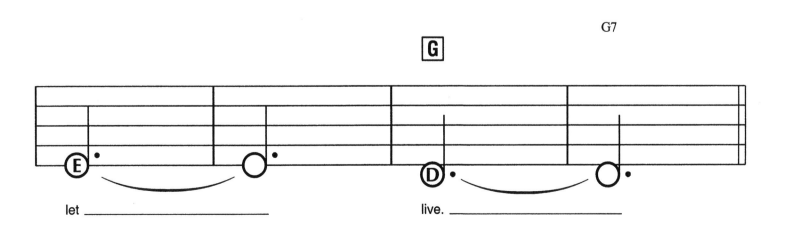

let _____   live. _____

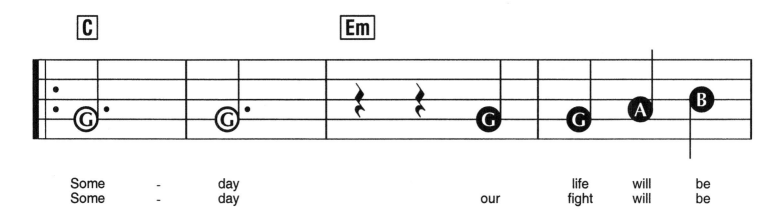

Some - day   life   will   be
Some - day   our   fight   will   be

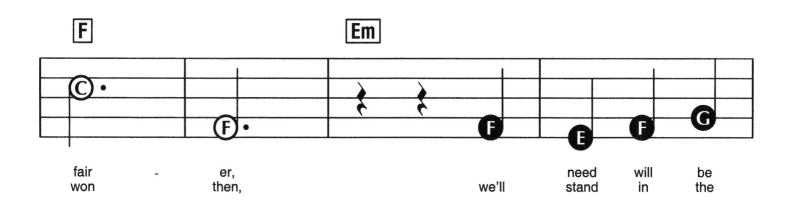

fair - er,   we'll   need   will   be
won - er, then,   stand   in   the

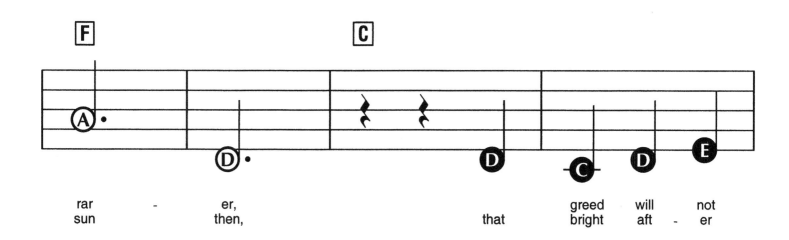

rar - er,   greed   will   not
sun - er, then,   that   bright   aft - er

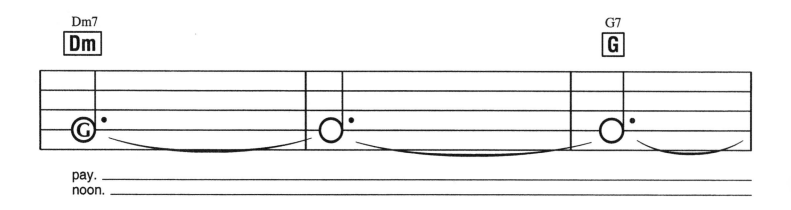

pay. _____
noon. _____

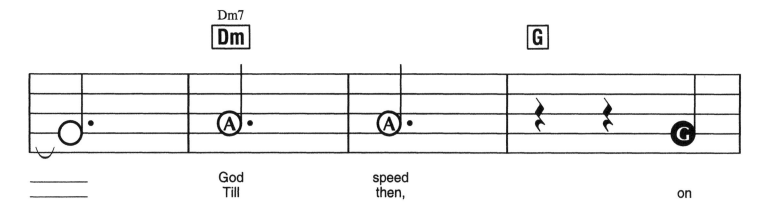

God speed
Till then,
on

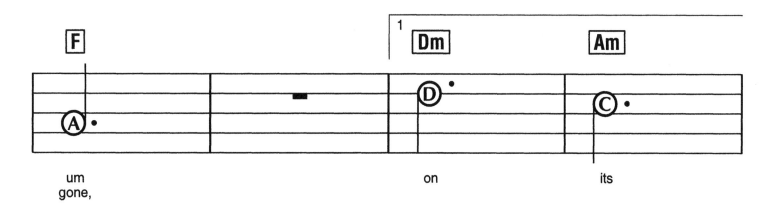

this bright mil - len - ni -
days when the sun is

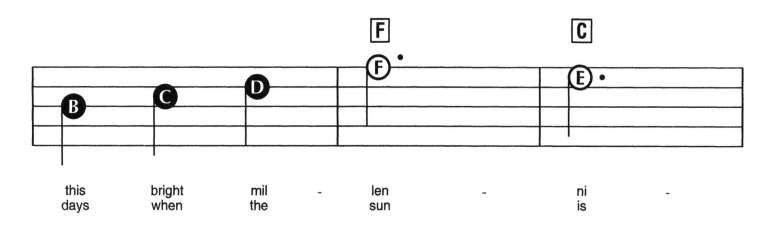

um on its
gone,

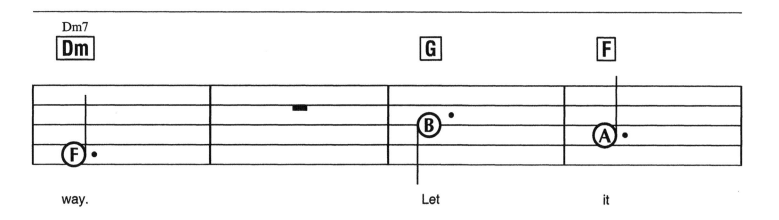

way.
Let it

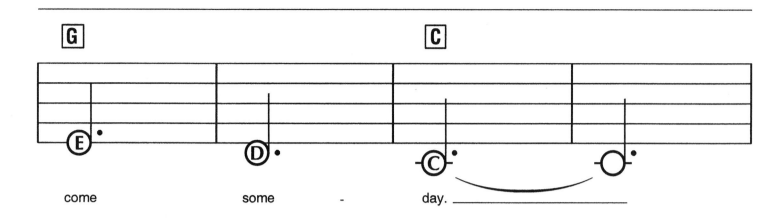

come   some -   day. _____

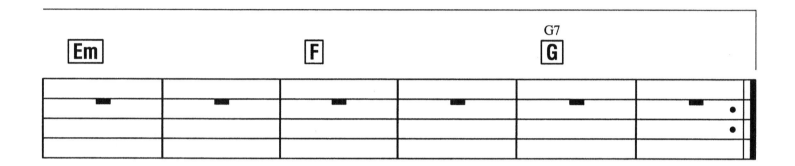

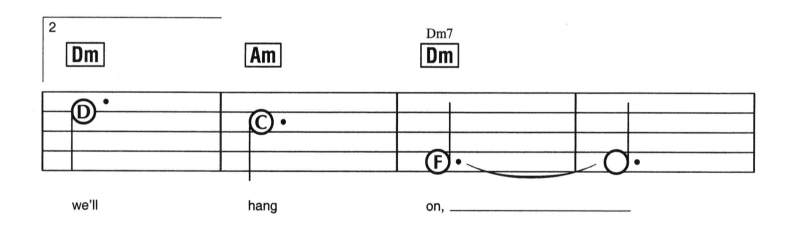

we'll   hang   on, _____

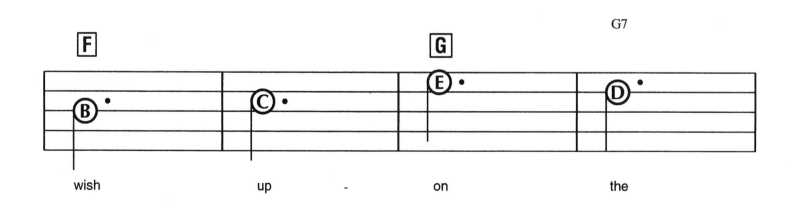

wish   up -   on   the

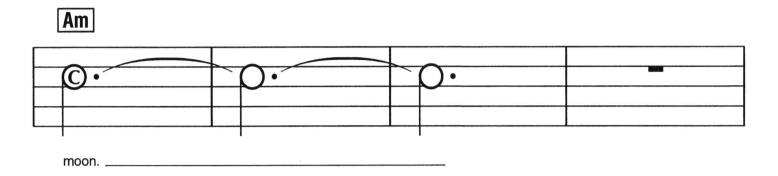

moon. _____

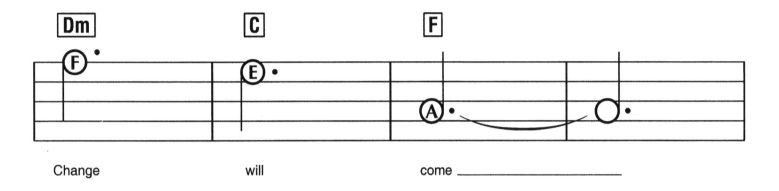

Change   will   come _____

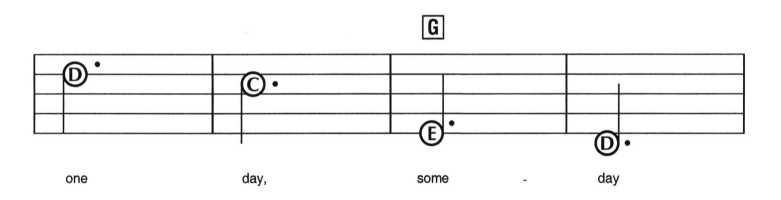

one   day,   some - day

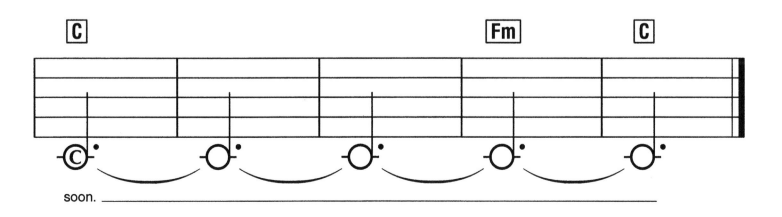

soon. _____

Supercalifragilisticexpialidocious
from Walt Disney's MARY POPPINS

Registration 5
Rhythm: Fox Trot or Swing

Words and Music by Richard M. Sherman
and Robert B. Sherman

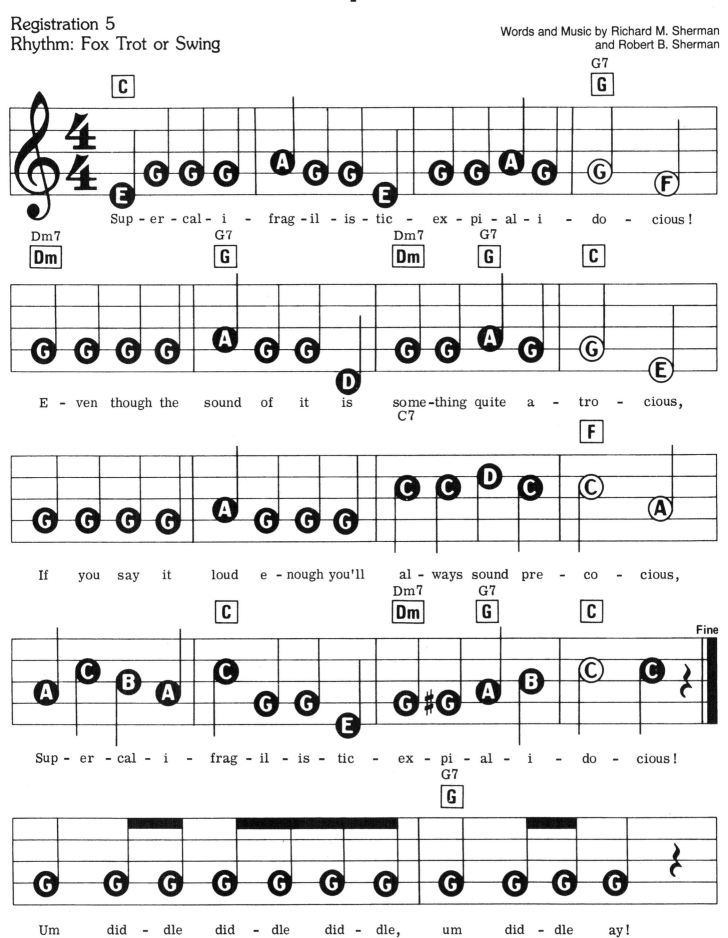

43

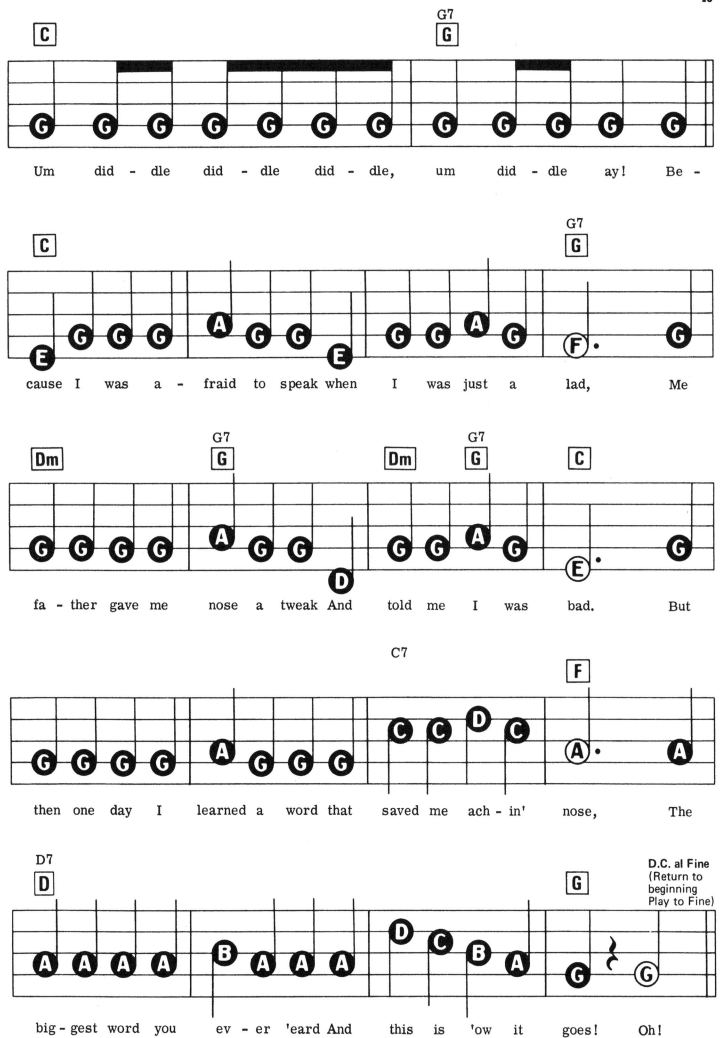

Registration 1
Rhythm: Swing or Jazz

Tomorrow
from the Musical Production ANNIE

Lyric by Martin Charnin
Music by Charles Strouse

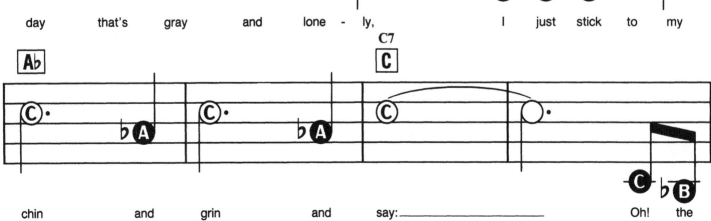

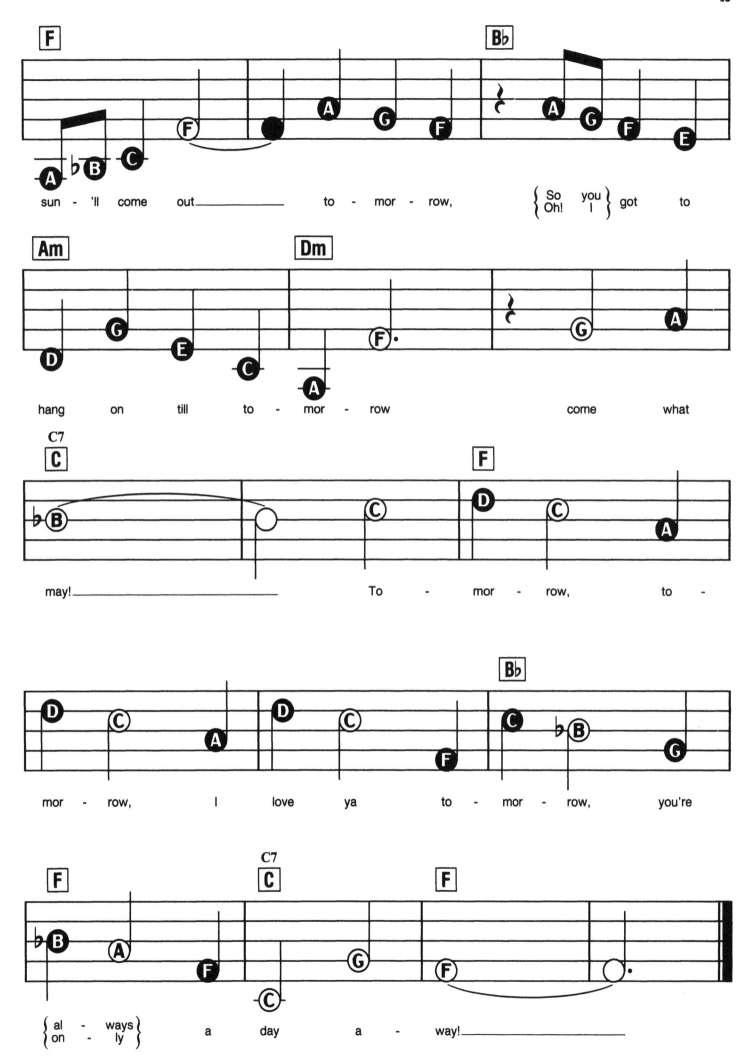

Winnie the Pooh
from Walt Disney's THE MANY ADVENTURES OF WINNIE THE POOH

Registration 2
Rhythm: Fox Trot or Ballad

Words and Music by Richard M. Sherman
and Robert B. Sherman

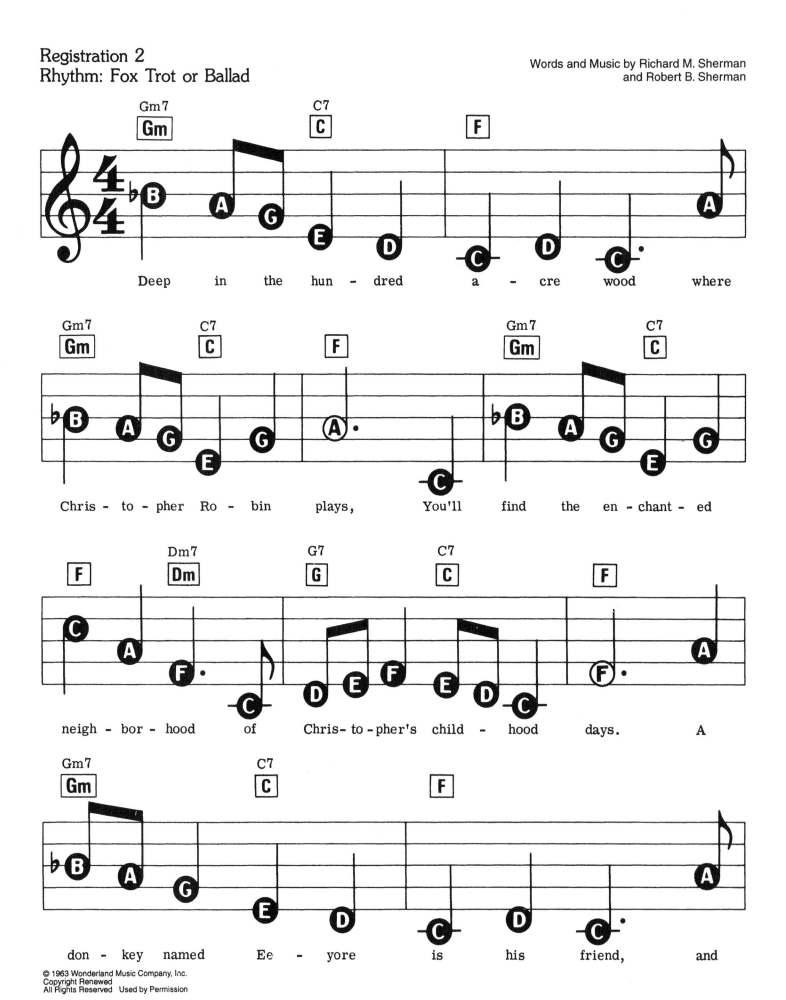

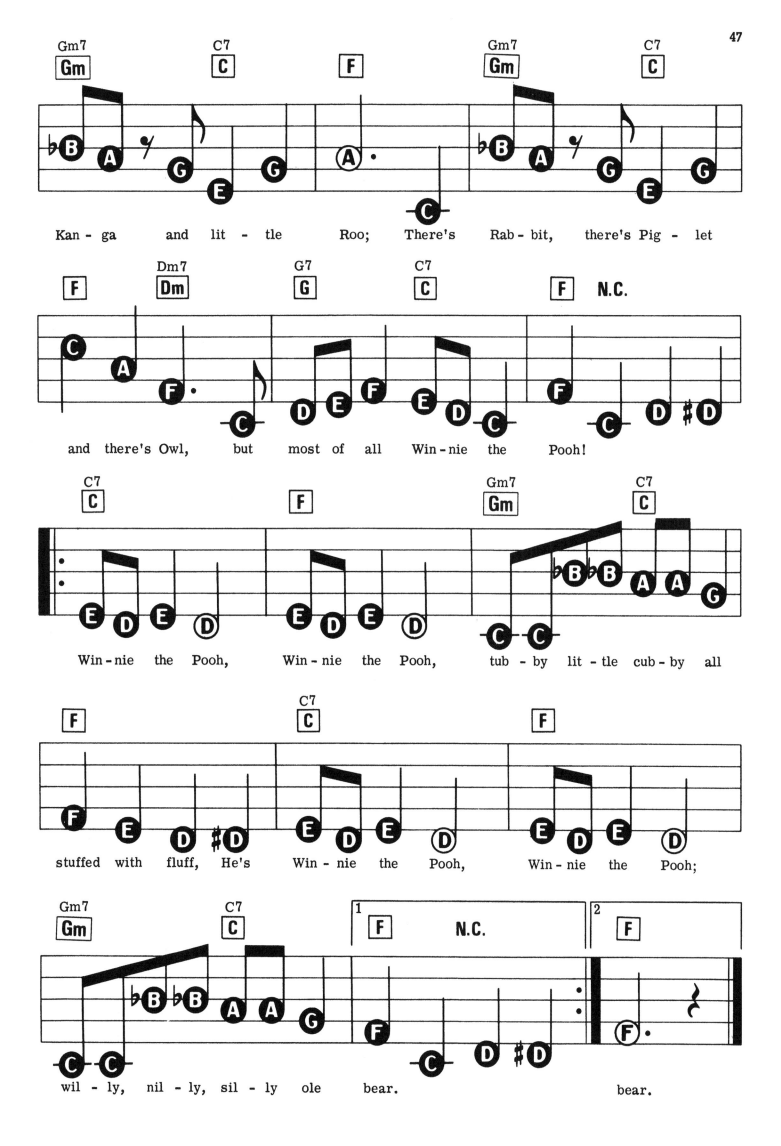

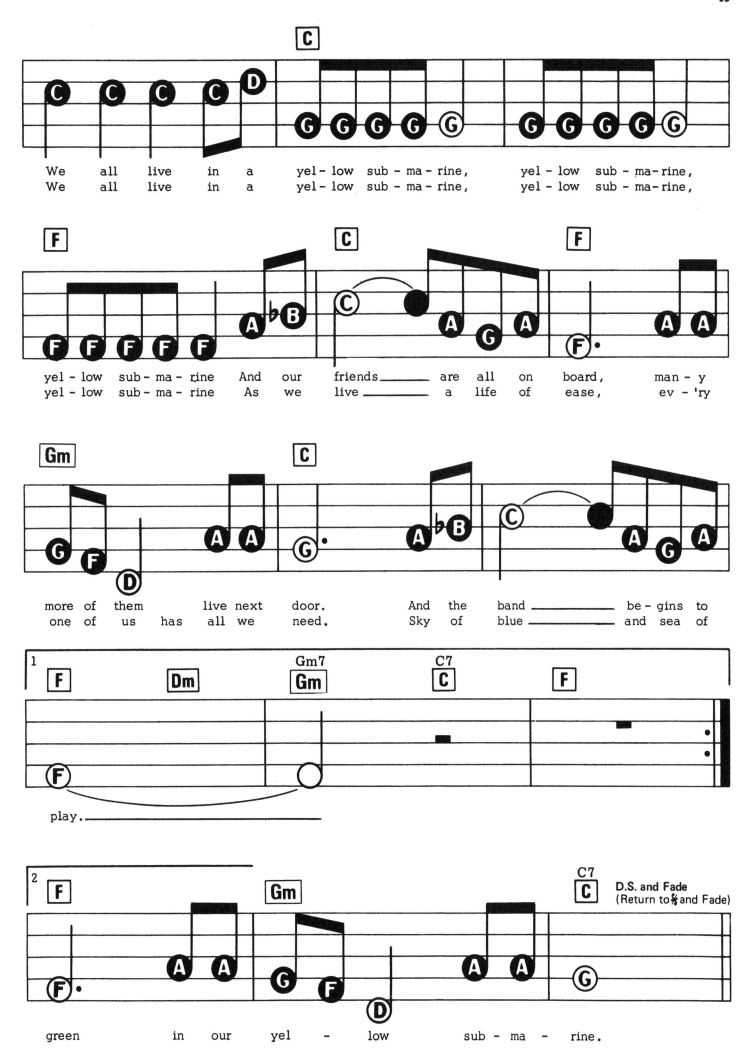

You'll Be in My Heart

(Pop Version)
from Walt Disney Pictures' TARZAN™
As Performed by Phil Collins

Registration 1
Rhythm: Rock or Pops

Words and Music by
Phil Collins

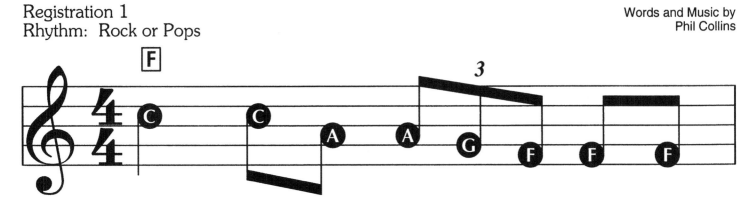

Come stop your cry - ing; _____ it will

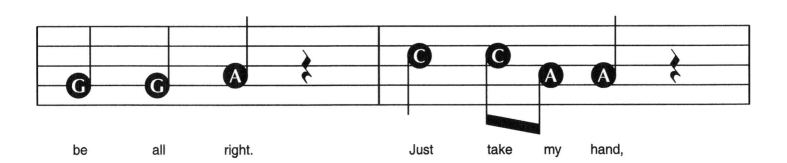

be all right. Just take my hand,

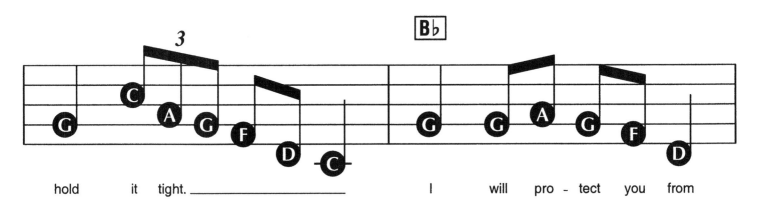

hold it tight. _____ I will pro - tect you from

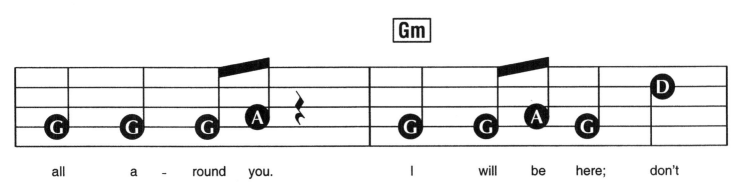

all a - round you. I will be here; don't

52

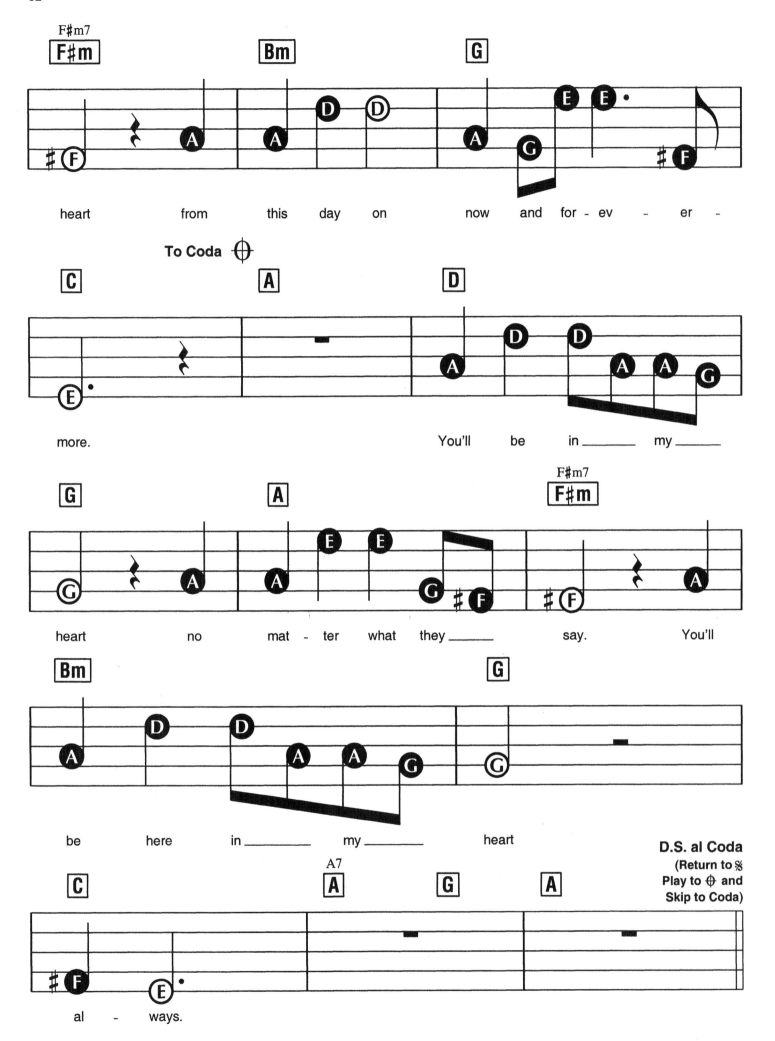

CODA

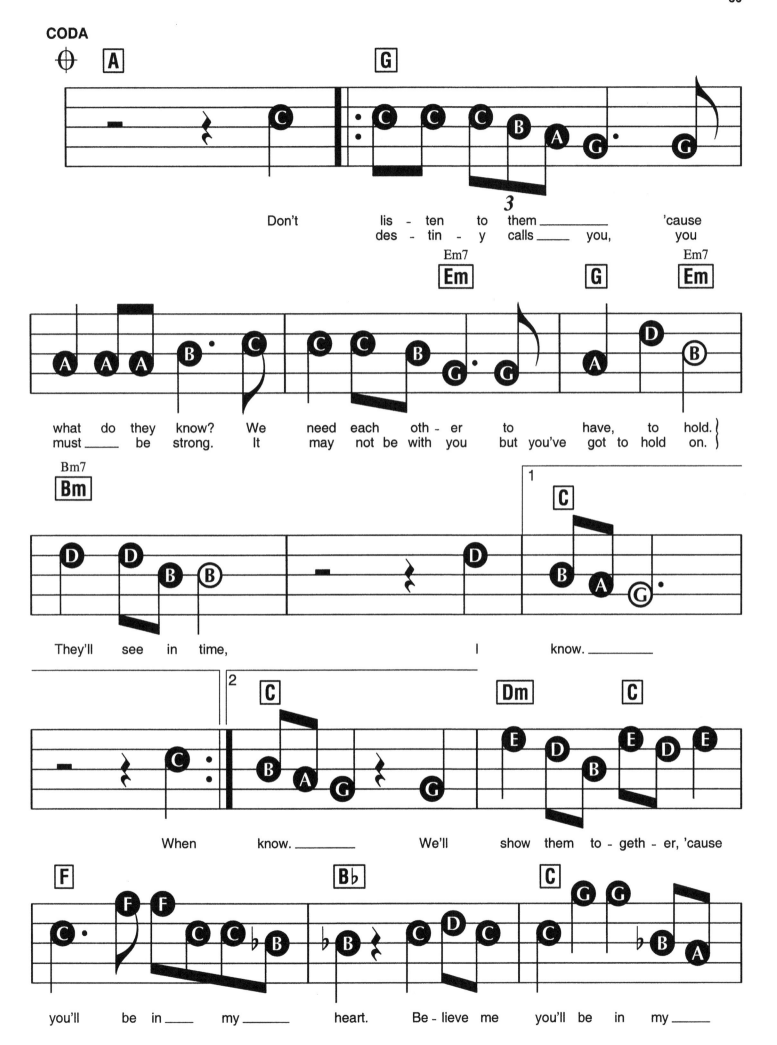

54

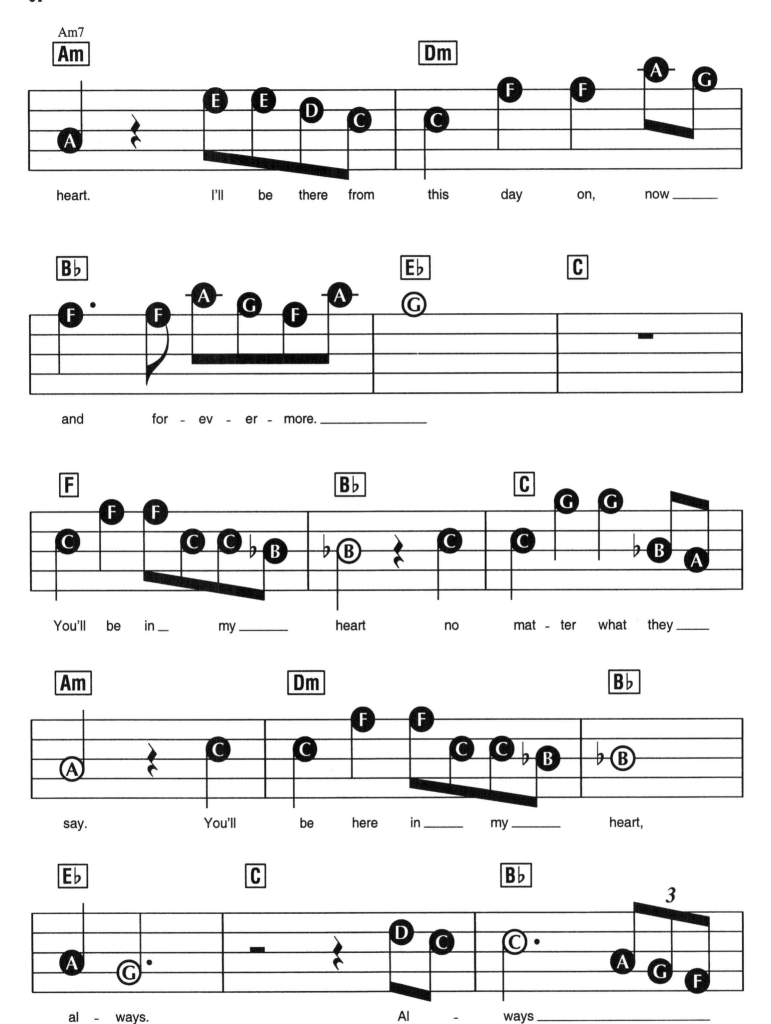

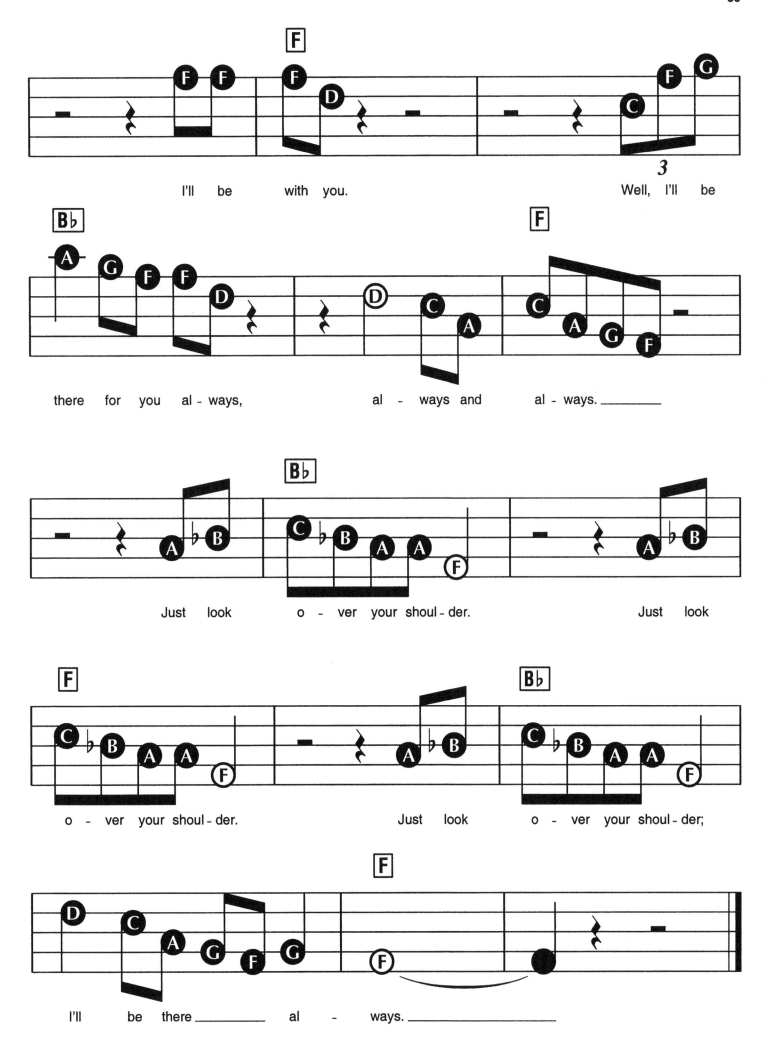

Registration Guide

- Match the Registration number on the song to the corresponding numbered category below. Select and activate an instrumental sound available on your instrument.

- Choose an automatic rhythm appropriate to the mood and style of the song. (Consult your Owner's Guide for proper operation of automatic rhythm features.)

- Adjust the tempo and volume controls to comfortable settings.

Registration

1	Mellow	Flutes, Clarinet, Oboe, Flugel Horn, Trombone, French Horn, Organ Flutes
2	Ensemble	Brass Section, Sax Section, Wind Ensemble, Full Organ, Theater Organ
3	Strings	Violin, Viola, Cello, Fiddle, String Ensemble, Pizzicato, Organ Strings
4	Guitars	Acoustic/Electric Guitars, Banjo, Mandolin, Dulcimer, Ukulele, Hawaiian Guitar
5	Mallets	Vibraphone, Marimba, Xylophone, Steel Drums, Bells, Celesta, Chimes
6	Liturgical	Pipe Organ, Hand Bells, Vocal Ensemble, Choir, Organ Flutes
7	Bright	Saxophones, Trumpet, Mute Trumpet, Synth Leads, Jazz/Gospel Organs
8	Piano	Piano, Electric Piano, Honky Tonk Piano, Harpsichord, Clavi
9	Novelty	Melodic Percussion, Wah Trumpet, Synth, Whistle, Kazoo, Perc. Organ
10	Bellows	Accordion, French Accordion, Mussette, Harmonica, Pump Organ, Bagpipes